GAY SPIRIT

A Guide to Becoming a Sensuous Homosexual

GAY SPIRIT

A Guide to Becoming
a Sensuous Homosexual

By David Loovis

A Strawberry Hill Book
Published With Grove Press

Acknowledgement is made:

To Judy Klemesrud and *New York* magazine for permission to use material from
her article "The Bisexuals";

To Random House, Inc., for permission to quote from William Faulkner's *The
Wild Palms* © 1939, renewed 1967 by Mrs. William Faulkner and Mrs. Paul
D. Summers;

To the Viking Press, Inc., for permission to use "Indian Summer," from *The
Portable Dorothy Parker* © 1926, copyright renewed 1954 by Dorothy
Parker; and to Gerald Duckworth & Co., Ltd., (Duckworth London) for
permission to quote "Indian Summer," which appears in *The Collected
Dorothy Parker*;

To Harcourt Brace Jovanovich, Inc., for permission to quote from E.M.
Forster's essay "What I Believe," from *Two Cheers for Democracy*;

To Macmillan Publishing Co., Inc., for permission to quote from Sara
Teasdale's poem "Barter." © 1917 by Macmillan Publishing Co., Inc.,
renewed 1945 by Mamie T. Wheless;

To Houghton Mifflin Company for permission to quote from Jessie B.
Rittenhouse's poem "My Wage," which appears in *Door of Dreams*;

To Vanguard Press, Inc., for permission to quote from *Auntie Mame* (Reprinted
from *Auntie Mame* by Patrick Dennis, © 1955 by Patrick Dennis).

ISBN: 0-8021-0076-7
Library of Congress Catalogue Card Number: 74-16593
First Printing
Manufactured in the United States of America

A Strawberry Hill Book
Published With Grove Press

Inquiries may be directed to Strawberry Hill Publishing Co., Inc., 230 Park Avenue, New York, N.Y.
10017, or to Grove Press, 53 East 11th Street, New York, N.Y. 10003

For Ed
who stayed close

OTHER BOOKS BY DAVID LOOVIS
The Last of the Southern Winds
Try For Elegance

*"Nothing but the senses
can cure the soul."*

–Oscar Wilde

Contents

GAY SPIRIT

A Guide to Becoming a Sensuous Homosexual

RIGHT ON

Dennis fondled my ear. I ran my hand over his stomach. We were still in bed together. We had just had sex.

"You were sensational," he said.

His remark delighted me, but it did not surprise me. For the last six years, my bed partners have been telling me that I'm sensational, fabulous, sexy as hell, the best they've ever had. In short, they didn't know before they met me how fulfilling gay sex could be.

Those compliments are no accident. I have done something special in order to deserve them. I have become a sensuous homosexual human being.

Some of my past lovers are among the most effective people in America—a Broadway producer who brought to the stage one of its most dashing female characters; a minister who has helped thousands with his TV sermons; a college president who guides the education of tender minds; a restaurateur with an international social clientele. Also among my lovers (at one time or another): a much-courted sailor in Norfolk, an always-booked-up hairdresser, a whiz exterior designer of formal gardens, a computer-brained corporation lawyer.

Yet the truth is, I'm not especially handsome. My face is pleasant and plain. I weigh in at 149 pounds and I'm five-foot-seven. My hair is brown with a touch of gray. I have the hint of a double chin and a pronounced stoop. My eyes are light blue with a slight cast in the left one.

I own no Bill Blass jackets or Gucci shoes. I wear a white shirt and a business suit to work, and in the evening a blue blazer and white turtleneck.

At parties and bars, I can express myself but I have no overpowering line. More often than not, I stand in the back.

I am that typical, quiet, decently dressed and well-mannered man who lives by himself in the apartment across the hall. My neighbors know that I have male friends who come and go without fuss, and a discreet party occasionally. I'm certain that they think me a kindly bachelor, which means to them a sexually deprived dummy. They take pity on me (pity in their estimation) and invite me to their parties, where all the males and females ogle one another and talk sex, but nothing happens.

Meanwhile, this kindly bachelor is having more and better sex than they could ever dream of.

For with determination and effort, I have learned to be a sensuous homosexual. Which is the very thing almost every bed partner wants . . . more than looks, dinners out or witty conversation. It satisfies them beyond riding in fast cars or lolling about a luxurious pad. It satisfies them so much they always come back for more.

Enticed by my sensual aura (Chapter 4), each bed partner of mine feels loved as he's never felt loved in his entire life (Chapter 12). I can make him feel as if he's discovering sex for the first time. After sex, I can cause him to get out of bed and feel he's entering a new and magically illuminated world. If you're able to do that for someone, you need little else.

I *can* do it, and *you* can too. You needn't have precise facial bone structure, be young, rich or wise, necessarily. You can learn to make your partner feel all those good things even if you are short, hairless and wear a truss. You *do* have to apply yourself to the exercise system, and to the techniques of erotic pleasure described later on.

You want to be a complete homosexual, don't you?

To find out how to satisfy your partner so magnificently that both your lives are enriched, turn the page.

1

GAY IS NEVER HAVING TO SAY YOU'RE SORRY

On June 28, 1969, the police raided a gay bar in New York's West Village called the Stonewall Inn. The event has been compared to the firing on Fort Sumter—homosexual liberation had begun. Instead of standing around and taking police abuse as they usually do, the gay crowd stuck together and fought back. They gathered outside the bar, tore up parking meters, threw coins at the cops, and outshouted them. The police took refuge in the bar and had to call for reinforcements.

From that day on, it has been the right time to be alive and gay in America.

Gay Activists Alliance got started. Colleges around the country recognized gay groups on campus and sanctioned their Saturday night dances. Gay publications sprang up everywhere advertising various gay services, as well as gay bars, baths and beaches. And most recently, the American Psychiatric Association reversed its stand and avowed that homosexuality is not a mental disease. A referendum vote later sustained the decision.

The Association's avowal—long overdue, ridiculous at last

and insulting as it is—is something. Fumbling, good-hearted America (when absolutely forced)—we love you too.

Never have gay people had such opportunities for expression.

You are the one who should be reaping the reward. Sex is easily available: brilliance on every street corner, divinity in the subway, gorgeousness in the supermarket. How lucky you are to be homosexual now. Gay is good today, proud, glamourous, peaceful, graceful, and more.

Time was in America when that was not so—in fact, the opposite. A boy at my college who combed his hair in a bang got chased through the dormitory, sheared and beaten. A friend lost his teaching credentials forever for being caught in the dunes rubbing sun tan lotion on his lover's back. Another attempted suicide with curtain cord when his mother found out. Oh, so short ago, gay was considered weak and evil and was cordially despised. That's past, thank God, that's past. In our new and hard-won freedom, however, we mustn't forget those times; we must do all we can to prevent slipping back.

Today, homosexuals not only feel freer, they *are* freer—and publicly declaring themselves. A friend of mine, a doctor, is still hesitant about coming out of his closet, so not everyone is free. He admits his fear but says the new gay movement warms his heart; give him a few years.

But so many gay people are shaping up.

Some, declaring themselves as totally gay—others as *bisexuals*. Cop-out? No, not if you have sex with both women and men. So often, gays make a declaration which seems to exclude women. It shouldn't and it needn't.

Straight people are shaping up, too. Exposed to gays in considerable numbers, they have made the surprising discovery that homosexuals are responsible, law-abiding citizens—and often talented. How tiresome straights can be; but give them a few years.

The effect of this recognition is curious: it puts the ball in our court. We've told the world that gay is good and beautiful and human and sexy. We've been heard. Now we've got to show we meant what we said. This is definitely not the time for doubts and fears and inhibitions.

So if you *haven't* been taking full advantage of the new gay scene—and you are gay—*you* have some shaping-up to do. Ask yourself if you're participating in all that emotionally enlivening, physically invigorating marvelous gay sex out there. Ask yourself if you have bed partners who are delicious at night, desirable by day, devoted to you anytime. Ask yourself if you have one person for your own who is your bridge to personal identity, as a lover can be. (Sex, that glorious uniter of opposites.) *If not*, then you probably have the same problem I used to have; it's high time to do something about it—as I did, and as did a number of my friends, with my help.

My problem began when I realized that a tumble in bed didn't fill the bill anymore. In my late teens, I'd gone through the usual/terrible business of coming out and getting adjusted to being different. Things went along O.K. for a while powered by the vigor of youth. Then this feeling of dissatisfaction began. First I tried to kill it with lots of sex; I reversed course and had no sex. But nothing worked; my responsiveness dwindled to near zero. Maybe, I thought, I'm experiencing early male menopause—even the delights I had known were to be taken from me. I went to a doctor. No, my physiological chart was excellent. All right, I needed a shrink. I went to an enlightened one; my psycho-sexual chart read out fine too.

What was this dissatisfaction, this conviction in me of unfulfilled potential? Very frustrating.

Deep unconscious logic kept nagging at me that somehow I hadn't become a truly sensuous homosexual, that I could give and receive ecstasy if only I knew *how*. I needed a key. The trouble was, nobody seemed to know much more about it than I. No—I must correct myself. I had some friends who were successful in the sexual arena; I asked them, but they hedged—damn it. I was furious, but who could expect them to reveal their secrets with so much competition around.

I pledged to myself that if ever I did discover the secret of becoming a sensuous homosexual, I would not hide it from others who needed to know. With this book, I'm keeping that pledge. Heaven help me if we're ever cruising the same trick! You'll know all my secrets! Oh well, may the best gay win.

The key to my dilemma came to me out of the blue in, of all places, Brooks Brothers. I had gone there to buy their funky dull ties, so characteristic of my pattern before my revelation (although I still wear them to work). I was on the main floor waiting for the salespeople to stop talking to each other and attend to me when the thought came, "I don't have to put up with this, I can go elsewhere." By that time, a salesperson had gotten to me. In particular, I wanted a maroon and blue striped regimental. The man went about producing it with what I considered a supercilious attitude. Again, I thought: "I am me, worthy of more than I'm getting here, more than I am getting anywhere—more than I'm giving myself! I must take hold!!" I decided not to buy the tie after the man had searched the piles and finally found one. I was too excited.

As I walked out of the store I saw the whole picture of how to take care of myself in a new way. How to tune my body's visceral sexual responses and, in consequence, how to attune my mind and become a complete and true sensuous homosexual. Strange that that small incident at Brooks Brothers should have brought into focus my new outlook, been the birth pang of my whole exercise system.

For that was the substance of my vision: the exercise system. I hurried home and wrote everything down. The hand of the muse seemed to guide my pen; it all came out at once and letter-perfect. But would it work?

With fear and trembling, I tried it. The first week, I felt better;

by the end of the first month, I looked better. At the end of four months, I began to radiate a sensual aura, and within six months my whole lifestyle had changed. I was giving and getting all the sex I could handle, and each experience was more incredibly wonderful than the last. Unbelievable! I had become a sensuous homosexual human being.

My next thought was that I must tell all my friends about it, especially the ones I knew were suffering the way I had suffered. But maybe, I reasoned, my exercise system is a fluke; it had changed my sexual life drastically, but would it help anyone else? Former advertising researcher that I am, I decided not to tell what had happened to me until I'd done some testing. Everybody noticed the change in me and asked about it, I just said, "vitamins." It wouldn't have been fair to get people's hopes up.

The first person I came across who seemed ripe for my revelation was Bob W., a friend of mine for ten years. Bob appeared to me to have everything: tenure at the college where he taught, a whole New York brownstone of his own, a car, a large circle of friends and, not least, good health. After one of his cocktail parties he asked me to stay and have dinner (I forgot to mention he's a great cook). Naturally, I thought we'd be three: Bob, myself and Bob's newest friend. But no, just us two. I chided him at the absence of a trick, with so many to choose from at his party, and I did a double take when he replied: "I just can't seem to get interested. I'm worried, upset, but . . ." And Bob faltered. Bob is one of the finest lecturers (his subject is sociology) in the country; for him to falter meant his problem was more than urgent—it was an emergency.

As we ate beef bourguignonne, I opened up to him about my exercises. I felt embarrassed about being so simple and direct to a man with such a complex brain, but he listened to me very attentively. Before I left that evening, I wrote down the exercises on a slip of paper and handed it to Bob.

Six weeks later, a jubilant Bob on the phone . . . "come to

cocktails and dinner.'' This time, instead of a confused and de-pressed man, there was Bob in the highest spirits, cooking away, with a new blond lover helping him. When the boy left the kitchen, Bob took out his wallet and removed from it the piece of paper I'd written on. ''This is a most valuable bit of literature,'' he said, and tucked it inside again. It worked, I thought; it really worked! ''Last night,'' Bob said, ''I came three times.''

Going home, all I could think about was that my exercise system had worked for someone besides myself. I really might have found the key to sensuous homosexuality. But one swallow does not a summer make. I'd have to test further.

I met Kenneth at an open meeting of one of those gay discus-sion groups, where a friend brought me because he considered it excellent cruising. Kenneth was tall, pasty-faced, with lots of hair. And lots of problems. He told the group about them and they were floored; nobody gave him a single piece of advice. After the meeting, when everyone was having coffee, I simply said to Kenneth gently that he might do well to see a psychotherapist. He told me he'd seen several his family had sent him to and it didn't help: except for these meetings, he preferred to stay in his room and not budge. I said I was sorry, we ex-changed names and phone numbers out of politeness. I went my way.

A week later—to my horror—Kenneth arrived at my place in a taxi with suitcases and several cardboard boxes. He said that I was the only one he'd talked to who seemed to understand, that his family had kicked him out, could he stay with me for a few days until he found a place and a job. Well . . . yes.

The first week was depressing for us both. He was looking for a job as a fashion designer; he'd been to school and his portfolio showed talent. I hoped he was good at something because he was dreadful in bed: the type that just lies there. He did say that his sex with me was no different than his sex with others, which is why he'd taken so much to his room.

I thought of my exercise system: would it work for someone with problems as serious as Kenneth's? I started him off. Two weeks later, still living with me and with no job, but medium good sex. A month later, still there, sex was wild and I was falling in love with him. Three weeks after that, he arrived home, (having been out seven nights in a row) and announced he'd found a job in his field, a lover and a place for them to live! And he thanked me for everything I'd done!

I was crushed, but gratified. You bet my system worked for Kenneth—even if it backfired on me.

Two more case histories—actually there were dozens before I started to write this book—and then we'll get down to the how-to's of the system for you.

Never mind where I met Rocco—but it wasn't professionally and if it was I wouldn't be ashamed of it. Anyway, here was this tough, hunky Forty-Second Street hustler sitting in my living room at a cocktail party, glowering at everyone. As I served him his tenth drink, he growled something about not understanding you queers, how can you like guys, etc., etc. He can talk, I thought, and I wondered if he could read. I asked him, and, in an offended tone he assured me that he could. Take this home, I said, handing him a typewritten copy of my exercises, and do what it says and let me know what happens. I've never seen Rocco again, but a friend who gets around a lot tells me Rocco is working as a buyer in a hard-sell department store, that he dresses ultra-mod and that he lives with a rich man on Central Park West. "Something came over Rocco suddenly," this friend told me. "In a period of a couple of months he changed. I saw him with the rich man at a ballet opening and he muttered the word 'exercises,' but I didn't get it and the crowd pushed between us."

I count Rocco as one of my greatest, if unacclaimed, successes.

My last example is not the same as the others; I offer it to prove that sensuality can bring happiness.

John T. was brought up by strict parents in a small city in upstate New York. John is not handsome, he has bulbous lips and a head of unruly black hair, and he's short. Not a tragic figure, but pretty sad. The only sex partners John had upstate were transients at the railroad or bus depot tea rooms. He longed for real love or even companionship. There was a local gay set led by an elegant (for that small town) man who owned the local movie houses, but that man, and consequently, the set, ignored John utterly. A really bad situation. John personally is a charming and generous and likable individual, but his worse-than-nil sex life was driving him to despair—and he was losing his good spirit.

So, at age twenty, John mustered his courage, said good-by to parents—kindly folks—and, with cash he'd saved from his job as YMCA publications director, he bought a used VW and set off for Florida.

You may not be aware of it, but Florida people are among the friendliest and sexiest in the nation, and a recent survey showed that Florida's young were the healthiest in the nation. If John was a flop at home, he was the star of that southernmost, sundrenched peninsula.

John settled first in Ft. Lauderdale, where, as you know, the boys really *are*. He got a job as a beach umbrella concessionaire, met the lifeguard and spent the most wonderful week of his short life. Second, he met an older man, an antiques dealer from Palm Beach. When John's lover-lifeguard paired off with another lifeguard, John went to Palm Beach to live with and work for the antiques dealer. Third, a customer came into the Palm Beach antiques shop, fell for John (now swarthy with the sun and thinned by swimming and sexing) at first sight, as John did for him, and off they went to Miami, where the man immediately began to train John to manage one of the restaurants in a chain that he owned.

In short, John spent that winter in Florida's beds—from Jacksonville to Key West, from Tampa to Dania—learning everything about pleasing and being pleased. Floridians adored his bulbous lips!

In the spring, John's mother fell ill, and with regret, he returned upstate. The gay set which had ignored John before saw and sensed the new sensual John, and two of them invited him to dinner. John accepted, went to bed later, and drove both people wild with excitement with what he'd learned in Florida. Did he go permanently with either one? He did not. He waited until the elegant movie-house owner who led the gay set called and literally begged John to come to a party. John went, and had sex later, but made no promises. The movie owner nearly had a nervous breakdown (drove around John's parents' house all night) until John went to live with him—and they live happily together to this day.

The lesson of this immoral tale is that John had the guts to get away from his family, his home town, to a place where he could discover his true sensuality. Then, others could see it in him. Only then could he achieve happiness.

No, I did not share the secrets of my exercise system with John. He, indeed, shared his secrets of getting bed partners with me. John is my idea of a truly courageous, self-aware, sensuous homosexual. And God Bless all of Florida, too!

Has my system worked for everyone who's tried it? No, of course not, I know of two people it did not work for. These two individuals told me in advance that they did not believe they could develop any further as homosexuals. If someone gives you a magic talisman, part of its good effect is the magic you see in it. First, they did not follow the system regularly; second, they did not believe in their own potential. No wonder they failed!

I know the whole idea of an exercise system to make you sensuous sounds strange, and before I came across it I would have had doubts about it if someone had presented it to me.

But I did come across it and it has worked for me and for almost all of my friends. It will work for you, if you let it.

Often, straight people believe that to be gay means to be a ravening sexualist. We know better; gay people can get stuck in their sex life just as do people who are not gay. *This book is to help you who are already homosexual achieve fullest gratification from being homosexual.* There is no need to despair any longer about being insufficient to yourself or others in the sex department. Take heart, hope is at hand. Turn the page and let's get down to the nitty-gritty!

2

YOU CAN LEARN, AS I DID, TO BE SENSUOUS

How can sensuality be approached systematically, you ask. And, won't I look funny doing "exercises"?

About looking funny. You look pretty funny now as you stand around at parties and bars in your hopeless state while all signs of personality drain out of you—and as you go home alone. You couldn't get to look much funnier. Yes, you may look a little funny to yourself in the mirror in the privacy of your room as you follow the system. But remember, most great enterprises look funny at the start: think of the mud-hole that is the foundation of a skyscraper, or the devastation that precedes a house undergoing renovation. You've got to begin someplace, and initial self-consciousness is a small price to pay for the transformation you are about to experience.

As for approaching the problem systematically, what do you think your brain is for?

Most of us learn about gay sex in the street, or worse places, and although street savvy is sharp, it doesn't cover advanced complications such as you have now. Now you've got to apply that gray matter and pull yourself above what you learned in the street, be restructured mentally to do consciously and better what you used to do unconsciously and, obviously, not too well. These exercises, plus my specific sexual instructions, (Chapters 11 and 12), will bring you to the higher mathematics of lovemaking. When you have mastered all of it with your brain, only then will you be effectively equipped to use your heart.

You've been submerged in a world that has been too much with you. These exercises are designed to recall you to life: reawaken in you an awareness of your five senses—especially your tactile sense. If performed precisely and regularly, these exercises will help change your dismal sexual encounters into golden moments of sensuality!

A word about false approaches—and I mean phoney props——things that gay people—mostly the young—do with and to themselves under the illusion of beautification. Such as taping up pectoral muscles, stuffing impossibly tight jeans with crotch wadding, using camp language accompanied by flying wrists, or wearing make-up, fluffy wigs. Very old-fashioned, but you can still find the type everywhere. If that is someone's bag, fine with me. But sensuous? Not really. Camp down the line; good for a laugh but not a lay. No, your sensuality will come not from props but from potentials deep within you. Your sensuality will be yours forever and not smudge or have to be removed——embarrassingly—as you climb into bed with some delectable trick.

With my exercise system you are on the road to attracting the right person for you with the sensuality that you are truly capable of, sensuality that you learn with your brain how to exude and to use in bed.

Three keys to sensuous homosexuality:
1. Recalling yourself to life.
2. Building your sensual aura.
3. Developing your sexual expertise.
In this chapter we will concentrate on No. 1, detailing the

exercises. The rest will follow.

No. 1 concerns your body.

You can't make love *without* it, yet it's amazing how forgetful we are of our chief stock-in-trade. Beyond youth, we tend to take the body for granted . . . have to, as we go about our jobs, clean our living quarters, cook our meals. Not only is our body taken for granted, it is allowed to slip downhill. That means when you eat that extra scoop of ice cream or can't resist that jelly dough-nut. Your body—after a while you find you can't make love *with* it!

Fortunately, the body—through will power on your part—is subject to moulding: actual physical change of curves and con-tours. I said through will power. I want you as of now to think sensuous. Which means think surfaces and sensations across those surfaces. Yes, you are now to become a sensationalist and utterly narcissitic: recalled to life!

EXERCISE 1

Take off as many clothes as you feel comfortable without. Turn on the radio to a rock 'n' roll station. Within reason, adjust the volume high enough so that you feel bathed in sound. Stand in a place where you are free to move around. Now, move it! Shake as though lightning hit the top of your head! Hands and arms going, hips gyrating, knees knocking and bumping. Let it all hang out! No dance steps, please—this exercise is to shake your blues away, to make you loose as a long-necked goose, get that tired tension out of muscles you forgot you had! Keep moving around, shed your uptightness on the floor, ooze it from every pore (don't forget to open your mouth just as wide as it'll go). You should keep this up for two three-minute periods. (You've gone longer at "Le Jardin," "The Tenth Floor," and other, lesser, cha cha palaces.) This exercise is also meant to give you an enlivened sense of your body as a whole. When you go into a bar, you go in as an entire unit, not just as a limber jaw or elastic anus. Blood rushing around? Marvelous. Stop for five in a chair. All right—prepare yourself mentally for "the bath."

EXERCISE 2

No ordinary bath, this. Come on, break out your best towels and that box of fragrant French soap you've been saving. Sink way down in a tubful of medium-to-hot water til only your nose shows. You can approximate the beneficial effects of an expensive whirlpool bath simply by keeping the water running while you soak. Using your neck and feet as support, undulate your body in the tub—lift that pelvis til your genitals emerge, then drop back down gently. Stay there for twenty minutes. Then turn on the cold water, and enjoy it as it lowers the water temperature to a refreshing cool. After exercise 1 (I hope you remembered to turn down the radio), here in the bath, you should not have a tense muscle. This is an excellent time to masturbate. (I'll talk about masturbation in greater detail in Chapter 3.) With prudence—because you're relaxed—stand up and take a shower, adjusting the water temperature to warm again. This warm/cool variation is proven therapy. Soap up, splash, wash your hair (Chapter 4), turn the water to cool again and then off. And quickly out and into the folds of that luxurious deep-pile towel. Your bath—as often as you have the time for it—should be as ritualistic, and therefore sensuous, as a Japanese tea ceremony. Douse yourself with cologne (sprinkle a little on those clean and pressed sheets you're about to lie on) and to bed. Ah, doesn't that feel good? You're a pampered panther. Stretch each limb gently but firmly as far as it will go, then gradually let it return to its natural position. Lie there for a while or read or . . .

EXERCISE 3

Get up and put on a robe. Exercise 3 can be done when you

have the time. But it is best accomplished just after 1 and 2 because you are in a relaxed mood, which is to say, a mood of heightened sensory receptivity. Exercise 3 is to reawaken your sense of taste, sight, sound and smell, but most particuarly your sense of touch. Your conscious enjoyment of *that* during sex can up your enjoyment of the whole act by at least 50 per cent. Go back into the bathroom: put your hand on the spiggot fixtures--how wonderfully cool the metal is even if the day has been hot. And feel the tile beneath your feet . . . though it's hard as stone, the touch of tile is soft, soothing. Back to your room, noticing the pleasant sensation of wood flooring or carpet. Pick up a book, preferably a new one. Open it in the middle, hold it against your face and breathe in—intriguing, the odor of paper, print and glue. Go to the bureau where you keep your shirts and underwear and, with your eyes closed, feel the difference between the downy cotton of your skivvy shirts and briefs, and the smooth elegance of your broadcloth or silk shirts. And to the closet where your dungarees are hanging. That rugged yet velvety surface of worn denim—nothing like it; bury your face in it. And last, go to a mirror and regard yourself. Pick out your good points: those eyes that have lured so many, those lips that have met other lips in wild abandon. Be totally narcissistic here, you're only alive once to enjoy yourself with what you were given—be rightfully proud of it. Now to bed again and lull yourself to sleep with memories of the best sex you ever had—and to dream, knowing that even better than that is yet to come!

EXERCISE 4

Here's a quickie. Find a pigeon. Yes, I said pigeon, the bird kind. As it walks, observe closely the movement of its head: back and forth, back and forth. Go home, take off your shirt, and imitate the pigeon's head movement. It is the particular exercise in preparation for sucking a penis. Try it in a series of five sets, then stop, five more, stop—until you are able to do the exercise with ease a hundred times. I realize that the excitement of the real thing will set off your adrenalin glands and give you the strength to go double that number, but without the real thing, one hundred is sufficient practice for the neck and throat muscles.

EXERCISE 5

No matter how much finesse you bring to the act of sucking a penis (Chapter 12), you will always encounter a partner who simply must have greater pressure on his penis than your mouth provides. Short of anal penetration or his penis in your armpit or between your jaw and neck or merely between your legs, you must use your hand and arm to work him up. It is my observation that gay sex often fails at this point, for the strength of the partner who is doing the working up is not sufficient to the task. It does require strength to maintain a steady hand pressure on the penis while increasing the stroke speed. Therefore, a specific exercise for the hand, forearm and upper arm: pretend you are shaking a cocktail. Use any glass or jar the size of a cocktail shaker if you haven't got one handy. Grasp the beaker at the top with one hand and at the bottom with the other, hold it high and shake it! Keep going steadily at this for one whole minute. It's tough. Now switch the position of your hands and shake away for another minute. Repeat this exercise several times until you can actually last five minutes without stopping. With the resilience your hand and entire arm develop from this exercise, you may save a difficult sexual experience from disaster.

EXERCISE 6

In Chapter 12 I will deal with the two major forms of homosexual intercourse: oral and anal penetration. You know them, but I will have some suggestions to offer in that chapter which will promote you from the status of casual performer to that of virtuoso. Meanwhile, as regards anal intercourse, with yourself as the receiver, let's concentrate on an exercise to improve your work in one of the basic positions, which is on your back with your legs in the air. It is very off-putting to your partner who is about to penetrate you for you to have to grunt and groan, or even creak and crack, as you assume your stance. So—lie down on the floor with one pillow under your neck and another under your buttocks and, legs up, pretend to pedal a bicycle. During the actual sex act, your hands will be caressing the head, chest and shoulders of the body lunging over you, but for now, place them flat out by your sides to give you leverage as you pedal that upside-down imaginary bike. Stop after two minutes and take a breather, then back up again, remembering that with a really good partner you might have to maintain your legs aloft for ten or fifteen minutes. All right, on your feet, and lean over the arm or low back of a chair, bracing yourself solidly with your arms as, once again, your partner who is behind you lunges in. Move your buttocks from side to side gently. Develop a slight rotating motion of the buttocks (not too much or you'll lose him). And while you're leaning over there, don't forget to hold your belly in as firmly as you can—awful for him to look and see a cowlike udder.

EXERCISE 7

Get a cushion. Bed pillows are too soft, so try a couch cushion for this, fairly large. Take the cushion and hold it straight out from your chest. Now, gradually slipping your arms around it, hug it to your chest. Repeat this five times. No clutching or grabbing motions; everything as gradual and rhythmical as you can. This is a preparation for that first embrace and kiss with someone you really like. The point is to eliminate any sort of jerkiness which he might interpret as nervousness or, worse,

over-anxiousness. O.K. Up to this point that cushion has been just a cushion; picture it now as that groovy guy you saw at the bar last night (who left with that little blond queen before you even had a chance). Picturing him, bring the cushion gradually toward your chest, embrace it, squeeze it tight, really hard, with everything you've got—imagining you can feel his body against you, his erection against your leg. Loosen your hold, change your grip on the cushion and again, hug it to you with a vengeance. The idea behind this exercise must be expanded to every tiniest movement of the sexual act. You must appear—and be-
—deliberate, confident and emphatic. No weak or spasm-like gestures. Part of your sensual aura is to exude firmness and whole-heartedness. This must reveal itself when you walk into a party or a bar, by the way. Don't sidle in uncertainly; enter like a full homosexual human being, with verve and space around you. That's sensuous!

EXERCISE 8

I do not minimize the effort required for No. 8. But I believe you will thank me for making you do it; it will enable you to perform oral or anal intercourse with maximum efficiency while looking quite good. We're concerned here with the abdomen and lower back muscles—areas where you must be a powerhouse. Pretend your friend is on his knees in front of you or on his back below you, with his legs in the air. Either way, you are expected to—and will be respected only if you can—give it to him good. A spongy, loose-folded rubber tire girdling your middle is not only obscene, it is a show-stopper in the worst sense. That much flesh takes a disproportionate amount of your energy just to move, not to mention maintain. Your strength is sapped and your ability at intercourse lessened. So, down on the floor flat on your back, with your feet hooked under some substantial piece of furniture, hands clasped behind your head. Yes, sit-ups. (I hear you groaning; it can't be helped.) Do two sets of seven to start. Work up to the time when you can do four sets of seven without being winded. This is one of the few exercises that you can observe results from in the first two weeks. Someday, when his hands are wandering lustfully around your hips and pelvic region, and you're on top pumping for dear life, you'll remember that I put you through the sit-ups, and you'll be grateful.

EXERCISE 9

The tongue, tongue, tongue: moist tendril of delight! Yes, the tongue is where it's at when it comes to your success as a sensuous homosexual. Amazing how much literature there is on the use of the tongue for sexual purposes. (Lest you think I haven't done research.) Every writer about the tongue idealizes it, has his theory about it. Me too. I am impressed with its versatility: at times used sparingly (for French kissing), at times gluttonously (analingus). But let me save that for my chapter on technique (Chapter 11). Now, I want you to obtain a slightly over-ripe but undamaged peach, and an old bath towel. Fix the towel around your neck like a bib. Hold the peach at point-blank range in front of your mouth—stick out your tongue at it fifty times. Then fifty more. You'll be eating that juicy peach in a minute or two, but just lick it first (oh that soft fuzz). Lick it twenty times, interspersed with tiny kisses, as if it were the fuzz on the inside of your partners thigh. Break the skin a little with your teeth. Put your tongue in the wound as if it were a healing syringe. Lick firmly, breaking the skin further. Lick with avidity as if the meat and nectar of this peach was about to be taken from you! Lick harder! Bite into it voraciously as you slowly squash the fruit between your hand and mouth, letting it mash soggily but sexily across your chin and as much of your face as you can. (Careful of the pit, of course.) With the meat of the peach, and the juice of it, all over your face, you are united with the peach, the peach is you—exactly as you will be united soon with your lover! Clean up with the towel. Vary No. 9 with grapes, plums, etc.

EXERCISE 10

Masturbation. But this requires its own chapter, which is next. Read on . . .

3

MASTURBATION

The fact that women masturbate was newsy until recently. The fact that men masturbate has been accepted for some while. The fact that men who are gay masturbate . . . well, we are connoisseurs of the art. I suppose it's been the result of the lonely life, the relatively isolated existence most of us were forced to lead until a few years ago. Talking about masturbation to gay people, then, is certainly carrying coals to Newcastle. But we can all use a brush-up on fundamentals. I've included masturbation here as the tenth exercise.

For those of you who happened to have been living in an abandoned mine shaft—yes, masturbate. There hasn't been a medical or psychological opinion against it in the last twenty years. The psychologist Wilhelm Stekel wrote a whole book in favor of it, which I noticed last year was widely circulated on the campus at Princeton (those Princetonians! they even have a special position named for them: Chapter 11). All the terrible tales your ancient aunt used to tell you as warnings against what she called "abusing yourself" are false. You won't grow hair on your palms or have double vision or walk funny. Masturbation is a healthy form of caring for yourself: an immediate way of being your own best friend.

There is one objection to masturbation which I feel I want to mention to you, but let's consider first the points in favor of it. And a how-to or two.

1. Repeat after me, loud and clear: masturbation relieves nervous tension better than aspirin, Bufferin, Anacin and all other similar pills combined. Sorry, but when it comes down to it, masturbation is even better than pot. Pot-masturbation is, however, like the Jackson Five or the singer Hildegarde —incomparable.

2. Masturbation is a superb way of getting and keeping the juices flowing. Your sex organs and glands (muscular compositions) will not enlarge by use but will certainly benefit from it. It is true that the sex organs forgetting, by the sex organs forgot! They can and do atrophy with disuse. But the fact that even the very oldest gentlemen have erections, especially in the morning, proves that sex never dies.

3. It is private—you really don't have to look your best—and it is quick, any john will do. Or it can be slow, if you wish.

4. It is uncomplicated, you need not take into account anyone's satisfaction but your own.

5. It is clean. Maybe a crusty little spot or two on your underwear, but you can cope. No possibility of a veneral infection.

6. Unless you are interrupted, it is thorough: climax is attained without fail.

All of that, in favor.

The how-to's of masturbation?

The ways are as numerous as stars in the sky. You could teach me a few, probably.

I have heard of bizarre ways: like while balancing yourself on your head and one hand, pseudo-yoga style. Like mixing it up between hand and penis with a piece of strawberry short-cake. Like straddling tree trunks, as did Van Gogh, I'm told.

The connoiseurs' method? Simple hand-to-penis. Stroke, tempo, pressure—everything under control. A vibrator is nice for titilation. And a porno picture book improves over-all performance.

About porn: I'm for it as an aid to erotic stimulation. The trick of getting the good of it is, to go slowly. The *conscious* mind responds to porn as you pick the dirty books off the shelf in the dirty-book store, which you leave with a brown paper bag and a hard-on. But the *unconscious* mind, where impression counts, takes longer to respond. If you've wondered why some masturbatory experiences satisfied you and others did not, that's the reason—you were going too fast for the *unconscious* mind to get the good of it. If you're inclined to rush, try a porno novel instead of the picture book; it may help.

About gadgets for masturbation: To me, they look fiercely complicated and off-putting, especially when there's electric current involved. But electric or hand-manipulated, they all work on the principle of suction; not dangerous, I suppose, and amusing possibly, if you're really into it. Gay people tend to send for the things, try 'em once and forget 'em.

Dildos are another matter. Flexible, made of weighted plastic, moulded and colored to look like the real thing, the dildo used in conjunction with masturbation is a worthwhile object. The prostate gland is massaged en passant and the orgasm is plentiful. You know better than to have to be told that objects like shoe horns, coke bottles, perfume stoppers, etc., have no business in your anus.

Speaking of the anus, I met a boy the other day who is able to control the muscles in and around his anal passage so that he can grip your inserted penis at any point; he can even undulate the pressure from base to tip and cause ejaculation without a move on your part! I thought only the female vagina knew how to do that. Live and learn.

Where to masturbate? Like Marcel Proust, most of us begin in the john over the johnny. Or, if you live in the country, in some grassy glade. Sometimes with other kids, sometimes not. (Sexy days—prepuberty—too easily forgotten: the first guilty thrill and all that.) Older, still in the john but more adventurous—in the bathtub. (I can tell you from personal knowledge that one of America's foremost living playwrights still masturbates by preference in the tub.) As an adult, if you are discreet, places to masturbate are legion, depending only on your ingenuity. Say, in your car parked at the beach while you watch a volleyball game. Or in one of the johns on a jumbo jet. Or, if you've got a coat to sling across your knees, in the waiting room of the bus terminal. Legion, as I said . . . I remember the john at Grand Central Terminal years ago. A line of at least thirty urinals . . . all occupied with people semi-masturbating. One person would come to a climax—and the whole line on either side of him would climax. Which illustrates for the benefit of your ancient aunt the adage ''work breeds work'' (Niagara Falls as the urinals all flushed simultaneously).

Summarizing, masturbation is a guarantee of an orgasm without tears—no emotional entanglements (but it doesn't add to your store of gossip, either). You're the boss so far as time, place and pace are concerned. It gets the gonads galloping for future use, and it's clean.

What on earth, you ask, could I object to about masturbation?

Smart people, gay or otherwise, do not masturbate every time the urge grabs them. That urge, good friend, is the raw stuff of psychic energy. It is the energy you require to push out into the world, to establish and maintain your human relationships, to do work that interests you, and to fight like hell when and if you have to.

To dam it up is difficult, I know. Makes you quirky, full of little compulsions and odd psychological projections. So masturbate when you must. But remember that without a certain amount of tension there is no personality.

Personality translated into sensuous terms becomes your *sensual aura*. And that aura—so important to you—is composed of three parts: grooming, dress, erotic role awareness (in the chapters coming up). When you've absorbed or acted upon the information in those chapters, you'll be well along toward your goal of becoming a sensuous homosexual human being! You'll be incredible!

4

BUILDING YOUR SENSUAL AURA

Two men cruised me at a party.

It was one of those really rolling, mostly gay parties. Guests came through the house and on to a firm sand beach. The sun, just setting, tinted gray-blue and pink a line of wonderful thunderhead clouds towering on the horizon (so characteristic of southern Florida). A luminous green sea, utterly calm, nibbled its way in. Torches, on poles stuck in the sand, flickered and fumed. A long, white-clothed hors d'oeuvres table . . . with silver candlelabra . . . platter after platter of food . . . a hill of toothpicked shrimp in the center. You would have enjoyed it.

Both men were in their mid-forties.

The first one spoke to me at the table. He seemed nice: he had good facial features, a little pale perhaps. He told me shortly that he did not like the sun. And then I noticed his eyes were red-rimmed and he did not look at me as he spoke. I looked at him; he wore a fussy jacket, all buttoned up. His hair lay dry and flat on his head. His voice, wan to begin with, dropped as our conversation faltered on, and I had to ask him to repeat himself. When he brought the conversation around to sex, he perked up somewhat.

A nice man but . . . well, you're getting the picture.

"I do all right," he said. "If I can get someone home. It's hitching up with people that I find difficult." He smiled through tartared teeth.

Small wonder, I thought, considering your appearance. O.K. in bed maybe. You *look* as if you were half-dead. I felt like grabbing him by both shoulders and shaking him and telling him to wake up. WAKE UP, MAN, AND GET WITH IT! LIFE IS NOW, AND TIME IS MOVING FAST!! TAKE CARE OF YOURSELF!!! Instead, I ate another shrimp.

He asked me to join him for a drink later.

I refused politely. This man's personal presence was not enticing. *He totally lacked a sensual aura.*

The second man came in late. I heard him tell the host he'd just arrived from New York, so he had no leg up on the first man as far as a suntan was concerned. His square-cut face was clean-scrubbed, a smile revealed bright teeth. He seemed, in general, poised for fun. I noticed that he wore his blue blazer open: the lapels rolled gently to mid-button. He had on white linen baggies and a yellow and white flowered shirt. He gave the impression of marvelous freshness. After he'd gotten his drink, and something to eat, his eye caught mine and he strolled over. (I think you can guess where this story is leading.) As he approached, I caught the scent of light cologne.

"How lovely," he said, indicating the wonderful clouds, only the top spires of which caught the last of the light.

We chatted. I noticed that he was gray at the temples, but that his dark hair had luster and he wore it in a natural, tousled way. His voice was soft, clear, edged with constant appreciation and delight. Everything about him said come hither. I hoped we would spend the night together. *He exuded sensual aura.*

What is that aura?

To repeat, it has three elements.

1. Grooming

2. Dress

3. Erotic role awareness

But if ever a thing was greater than the sum of its parts, sensual aura is. It's not flashy. You can't necessarily spot it quickly among people in a crowd. Seeing it is like observing a bright object—you must adjust your eyes. But once you've focused, the effect . . . uhmmmmmmm!

It is a freshness of everything about the individual. There is a throw-away elegance about his clothes. He moves easily; his body muscles seem toned but relaxed. And you feel that the blood runs true in his veins. He is quietly intense. His voice conveys self-regard and perception of others. You know sex with him would be memorable. (It was!)

Note: There's a difference between looking sexy, as kids do without trying, and having a sensual aura, for which you've worked. The first is fleeting and accidental, however charming; the second is yours for as long as you wish to maintain it. Sexy-looking kids may or may not be good in bed, like as not. But you, with your sensual aura, always are. And your prospective bed partner can sense it. That's what your aura is for!

To business: building your aura, step by step.

First, grooming.

Let's start at the top.

Hair

Barbers are called stylists today. A stylist specializes in not only cutting your hair so it doesn't appear newly cut, but also in helping you find a way of arranging it that is natural for you. Hair makes the man these days almost as much as clothes. Prospective bed partners will forgive a lot (ski-jump nose, receding chin etc.) if you can give them a good head of attractive hair to get their faces into. About washing: your hair does not have to be squeaky clean after every shower; you'll rob it of its oil—wash briskly when you do wash. Good shampoos are numerous; find a mild one. Here's some news: according to the gay chit-chat magazine ''David'' (the southeastern counterpart of ''Michael's Thing''), creme rinses are out. Their basic chemical structure is the same as that of permanent wave solutions: prolonged use tends to make your precious locks fragile and brittle. Reconditioners, as opposed to conditioners, are in (same source). I won't get technical, but apparently reconditioners contain the right chemicals to restore damaged hair (split ends—I hope you wouldn't be caught dead with a split end)—and mere conditioners don't. Questions? Consult your stylist. You should patronize one in particular so that you can train him right. A fella's best friend is his hair stylist. He'll advise you, of course, that a dryer is a most important bathroom fixture, but set the dial on *medium*, not hot; high temperature setting is another thing that robs hair of oil. I drive a lot and pick up hippie hitch-hikers, if they look decent; their packs are bulky because nine out of ten of them carry a dryer. Hair coloring? Why not: a touch to control a dingy graying, or, if you prefer, to highlight it. The products in this area are mostly good, and easy to apply. Don't get over-enthusiastic and change the color completely; besides appearing as if you dyed it, it makes your features hard. Massage your scalp regularly; a tight scalp is the prelude to baldness. Ditto excessive use of hair spray. A last word on arrangement: Sort of long is in, but if you try to imitate the kids and grow it to your shoulders, or let a goodly dollop fall over your forehead—you're out. Kids are for sex, not for imitating. Embarrassed by baldness? Get a hair-piece or wig. Many wear them by preference.

Eyes

You've heard that eyes are the mirror of the soul; it's especially true for gay souls. Often, gay eyes are expressive: they see, in contrast to eyes that only look. They also have a tendency to roam (too much exercise at who's-coming-in-the-bar-door). If you need glasses, get 'em, or contact lenses. Squint lines form fast, face lifts are expensive. Eyebrows may be trimmed if they meet in the middle, or curve downward too far at the outer side (unless the sad clown effect is your bag). Plucked eyebrows are an abomination. So is most eye make-up; I can't bring myself to say all. I have seen subtle treatment of the eyes that is compelling. But it requires the hand of a master not to overdo; also time to apply that might better be used cruising. Boric acid is the simplest remedy for those red rims after a heavy night. Rush to a doctor if you find any serious inflammation of the lids or eyeball. Always try to focus directly on the eyes of the person you're talking to. But if *his* eyes roam constantly, the hell with it.

Ears

You make think the inside ridges of your ears, especially at the top, are becomingly sun-tanned—other people can see it's dirt. In these days of long locks, golden or bronzed, a number of people haven't observed their ears since the "greening of America" began in '67. Not their ears, or the backs of their necks either. Upsweep your hair, and with soap and hot water and a washcloth proceed to cleanse those hitherto restricted areas. Unless you swim every day (lucky dogs), buy and use Q-tips to get inside your ears. Ears are a prime target of erotic pleasure. Inside, outside and in back, your ears want to be beacon lights that you're hiding—to unsheath at the dramatic moment when a searching tongue is homing! Be prepared.

Teeth

Your teeth must be perfectly healthy. I said perfectly. If you've noticed a black spot on one, get thee to your dentist; preferably, again, a man whom you see regularly and whom you trust and like. And have a cleaning at least twice a year; you know you need one when your teeth feel as if they're wearing little sweaters. Or look discolored—nothing is so off-putting, not to mention bad-breath-inducing. If you require elaborate work; begin. Most dentists are accustomed to time payments, if you're short of cash. Knowing that your teeth are perfectly in order adds immeasureably to your self-esteem; glowing teeth mean a brighter sensual aura. And it's true—the least indication of unattended teeth brands you in this day and age as profoundly neurotic. Remember that grungy number you almost asked home until he opened his mouth and showed you Death Valley! Any similarity between his mouth and yours mustn't exist.

Moustaches And Beards

Kept trimmed. You're not alone if you've discover that taking care of them is as much trouble as shaving every day. Remind your stylist to clip the hair tufts in your nose and ears; other people can see them even if you can't. About excessive body hair: a dark mantle over your shoulders and down the backs of your arms is not too fetching in bed or on the beach, although I admit some of your partners may like it. I don't on myself. Invariably, on my way south, I litter one Howard Johnson's motel bathroom with unwanted body hair; they give me towels, I leave them hair: fair exchange. A shave around the neck and top of my shoulders a few times a year suffices. There are sophisticated cremes to do the job; I've tried 'em; my hair grows back as fast one way as the other. I think kissing a beard and/or moustache is fun. Beard shapes are inventive. Beards do make you look older and some beards and moustaches even make the young look distinguished. It seems too bad to hide a handsome young face—there'll be plenty of later years for that. I think whether or not you wear them depends upon what kind of partner you're trying to attract (Chapter 10). I know one individual who has grown whiskers to discourage a lover he feels saddled with. And a pair of lovers who are delighted with each other's luxuriant growth (they resemble two birds in a bush peering out at you). Allen Ginsberg's beard is archetypal.

Facial Skin Care

Your face is the gift wrap on the prize package of yourself. Packaging is important these days. Unless you capture his attention, you'll never get into his hands, or pants, whatever. I'm for the use of skin cremes, regularly, accompanied by light facial massages (heavy massaging breaks down facial muscle tissue and it becomes flab). Check your face, especially your nose, for clogged pores. City living and a beachside existence dry out the skin. A swipe of baby oil or Bain de Soleil across your face each morning helps. Don't forget your throat—those little pimples you cut open shaving are there because your skin is flaky and/or your diet isn't balanced. Cremes that imitate a sun tan, never. If you live in the north, don't give up on the sun in the winter. There's nourishment in those rays even in February; bundle up and sit outside and you'll see. (Let them scoff—you'll have refreshed skin.) Unless you suffer from acute acne or terminal hickies, make-up is out. Make-up is for drag queens, bless 'em all.

Manicure

O.K. to keep the cuticle in shape. I guess I haven't had half a dozen manicures in my life. You can get one at your hairstylist's emporium. Elaborate, those places; I'm intimidated. High gloss? Undue length? Strange shape? No, no and no. I have yet to meet a pedicurist; I am my own and so must you be. Take care of those toenails.

General Body Care

Feet again; they do not automatically clean themselves when you shower or tub. Your feet want to be kissing-sweet. Attend to them with your fingers or a soft brush. Ablutions every day, needless to say. Deodorant soaps leave your skin fragrant, scaly and itchy: your druggist has better soaps for your skin. Basis Soap, if your skin is especially dry. There's cachet in using soaps other than the popular brands. It's the same as equipping your shower with an inner curtain as well as an outer one. Under-arm deodorant, of course. Powder or deodorant in the genital and rectal areas, absolutely. Tiny blemishes or ''skin tags,'' as the medical profession calls them, are not usually serious and can be checked by your doctor when you visit him for a pep pill prescription—makes your visit more legitimate. Sores or a rash I will get to in a minute.

Posture

I admitted to you at the beginning that I have a pronounced stoop. I do when I'm careless, which, granted, I should never be. But let a trick that I want enter my field of attention and you'd swear I'd been posture-trained at West Point! Posture is an indicator of your attitude toward life. Gay is proud, remember, so straighten up. As the Hunchback of Notre Dame, you will ring no bells with a bed partner. You can be your own pedicurist; you can also be your own chiropractor. Bow your arms as if they were wings and, with your head back, stand tall (you can often hear the spine snap into place). Standing tall also pulls the neckline taut in case you're starting to develop a double chin. And your clothes will fit better. So, tummy in, he may be looking your way!

Voice

A slurry, nasal, wan or swishy voice will drive lovers off in droves. Most people don't have the slightest idea what their voice sounds like. Do you? If not, get hold of a tape recorder and either talk or read something into it. Play back: if you sound unexpected to you, or if any of those aforementioned adjectives describe your voice, you've got a problem. Not a serious problem because you *can* do something about your voice. We are the daily target of great voices on TV. (Cronkite may look like a pipe-and-slipper man but he is no slouch when it comes to delivering a line.) So don't unconsciously judge yourself against old hands at the game; your voice is not that bad. What to do: *first*, remember to speak up, no mumbling in your martini; I have observed potential friendships abort because one of the partners couldn't get a sentence through the olives in his mouth. Mumbling makes you sound drunk or crazy, or worse—irrelevant. *Second*, slow down when you talk; it's amazing how people will pay rapt attention to a slow talker, while a fast talker's words zip right by them. It helps if you have something to say. But, *third*, even if you don't, try to appear as if you've given consideration to the words that pass your lips, being as precise as you can in their utterance. Your voice is the first real indicator of your personality that your new bed partner will encounter. Make it a lasso to draw him in, not a whip from which he'll recoil, or a wet mop he'll avoid or a star-spangled gay voice he'll be embarrassed by. If I had only one quality of voice to opt for, I'd choose *sincerity*. People who mean what they say and say what they mean are rare birds and when you run into one, that fact alone is compelling. Oscar Wilde said that ''shallowness'' was the sin of homosexuality. Some gay voices are shallow without meaning to be. Avoid any hint of shallowness by being and sounding as sincere as you can.

Voice (More)

Most gay people don't swish when they walk; it's curious,

though, how many gays allow themselves to swish when they talk. Their voices are constantly intoning ''my dear,'' ''baby,'' ''for days,'' ''darling,'' and (worst), ''get you, Mary.'' Sophisticated gay people may not use those phrases, but a kind of brittle joking often pervades their speech, without their being aware of it. Acerbic humor (being gay) is one of the better-known defense mechanisms, and gay people in America have had every reason to be defensive. But that's diminishing and it is to be hoped that verbal camping out of place will diminish also. (Girls' names for boys are permissible only in bars after midnight when you're very drunk.) So, three ''be careful's'': *first*, of vocal swishing- —become conscious of yourself in action, watch how off-putting it is, stop yourself. *Second*, of making humorous asides to an imaginary audience when you're actually talking to someone- —downright rude, if not nutty. And *third*, of letting your voice slide—drop in power, become wan in delivery (like the first man I encountered at the party).

Health In General

It always amazes me when someone says, ''I've had this condition for some time. I really must see a doctor''—in reference to a rash in the armpit or crotch area or anywhere, or in reference to chronic diarrhea or constipation, or in reference to inability to sleep, or a pain somewhere, or an over-all run-down condition. I feel like calling a cab and escorting them immediately to a doctor's. You cannot hope to achieve the degree of sensual aura you're capable of without an A-1 bill of health. And anyone reading this who has an inflamed lump on his body or a sore that won't heal, please drop the book and rush directly to a hospital. All the horrible things you've heard about the long-term effects of unattended cancerous growths and/or venereal infections are true! Cancer is curable in its early stages. If you are infected with VD it can usually be taken care of in a couple of visits to your doctor. Nobody is going to notify your boss or your mother, unless you've had sex with them, which is another can of beans entirely. And out of common decency, you want your lover, if you have one, to know and get cured, as well as any tricks you've had recently. If word gets round the bar where you hang out, you're dead anyway. Crab lice, or as the French call them more delicately, "papillons d'amour" (butterflies of love) and athlete's foot are remediable in one ten-minute application with drugstore stuff. Ditto trench mouth. Truss wearers: hernia operations are simple these days. Have yours now; you'll feel more together.

Vitamins and Diet

About vitamins, I am as confused and cowed as the next man. The drug companies would have us believe that the morning ingestion of a multiple vitamin pill is a sacred ritual. I do take one to be on the safe side (despite rumors and fads, no vitamin yet is a proven aphrodisiac—Chapter 16). And if I'm feeling hung over or coldish, I pop down a 500-mg tablet of vitamin C. If you've never been in a health food store, go and see. Just walking through one makes me feel better. About diet. No one these days can ever be too thin, so that's that. An overweight gay must eat less, exercise more (Chapter 2) and keep his bowels moving. That tidbit of information cost me hundreds of dollars and thousands of tears. It is the ultimate medical knowledge on the subject, truly. If you're capable of implementing that advice, daily and totally, you qualify for a hero's award. I have found its partial implementation some of the time is a possibility—with partial results, which are better than none. When you do eat, avoid food rich in preservatives, especially pre-boxed and baggied pastry: it repeats all night. There's junk food as well as junk everything else in our culture: amusing, sometimes tasty, but valueless nutritionally. Unadulterated should be the criteron of what you eat—things "they" haven't got their grubby hands on!

* * * *

And so—groomed!

Look in the mirror.

Isn't that an improvement!

Told you so; your caring about yourself is the prerequisite for others' caring about you. There's a just-visible glow beginning around you now—your sensual aura!

One caution: You can be over-groomed. The look is too perfect. It always seems to me that physically unhealthy gays overgroom themselves: plucked and pressed and pouty people—you've seen them. Stuffed-doll dummies with set-piece mask faces. If only they'd spend a little time exercising, you might feel there was some pulsating living tissue under all of it. Their clothes are designed to hide their bodies.

Your clothes are meant to enhance it.

And, speaking of clothes . . .

5

YOUR SEXUAL ROLE TONIGHT; THE GAY THEORY OF RELATIVITY

But before I talk about clothes . . .

I want to tell you something that may help you cruise successfully *tonight*!

This is gay uplift *shock* treatment; if it works, the end of your sexual dry spell will be hastened.

It does require searing self-honesty.

Plan to go out this evening, for sex.

Ask yourself before you go, what type of person would really satisfy you; fill that emptiness, get rid of your frustrations.

How about a little soft young queen? A boy you can kiss and cuddle with for hours, who will suck you practically dry, then willingly turn over and let you fuck him. A boy you can dominate.

How about a hunky, tough hustler? Muscles everywhere, legs that strain Levi seams, someone you can blow three times and who'll still have enough left to ram it into you. A hustler to whom you can be submissive.

I warned you this was shock treatment.

Those two examples are extremes. Your needs will lie somewhere in between.

But the thing is to *ask yourself very consciously what you're in the mood for*, then *go out and find it*—or as close as you can get. Believe me, whatever you want and need is out there.

Or, how about a soft-spoken, charming well-dressed older man who reminds you of your father (or the father you wish you'd had)? Someone you can talk to, tell your problems to, bring home or go with to his place and then—fuck the daylights out of, venting on him the fury and rage you felt against your real father for being so damned nice and remote. In short, dominating him.

Or, an older man again, this one coarse, but solvent and generous, and perhaps understanding of you without many words? A man who will take you home, wine you, dine you—even give you money!—and who will then proceed to ravish you; force you to suck him, force you (gently) to get fucked by him. To whom you can be submissive.

Yes, I'm touching on role-playing (the great taboo subject in gay life); yes I'm being very frank; yes, it does require a totally blunt, though temporary, self-evaluation.

I say temporary because, if it works, you may ask yourself tomorrow night what role you want to play and the answer may be exactly the opposite of the one you previously played!

Yes, this is shock treatment to break that sexual bind you've been in. It takes guts. It takes both calculation and discretion. And a willingness to experiment.

Or, how about someone your own age, whom you can talk to a bit, who you may feel has similar problems? How about going home with him and diving in—let the role-playing chips fall where they may! Maybe neither of you will dominate or submit or both of you at different times during the night will play both roles to your mutual satisfaction. A person with whom you are pansexual.

One reason this subject has been taboo is that gay people really don't like to admit to enjoying the submissive role, although the term "submissive" is just a term with no judgment attached. Let's stop and give this some thought.

Women's Lib and Gay Lib argument is based, generally, on objection to the fact that western civilization for two thousand years has taught people to admire certain so-called "male" characteristics and to be ashamed of so-called "female" characteristics. *That characteristics have any gender at all is a myth!* A male can cry and benefit, as only females are "supposed" to do; a female can run a business or hold office with the expertise that only a male is "supposed" to have. Pugnacity, emotionalism, physical endurance, submissiveness, dominance, self-effacement, detachment, hostility, gentleness, rage, sweetness—these words can apply to characteristics of either male or female.

The words "dominant" and "submissive" are apt descriptions of the two major gay sexual stances, but the terms are not intended as judgments. The terms, to repeat, are descriptive. Still, the subject of role-playing remains taboo—*for this reason*: "dominant" is mistakenly considered masculine and good, while "submissive" is mistakenly considered feminine and bad.

Foolish prejudices!

Submissive gays are ashamed of their need.

Dominant gays are absurdly proud.

Cool consideration of the matter flies out the window.

Takes honesty and joy with it.

And at last, the whole matter is undiscussable.

Another reason the subject of role-playing has been taboo is that it's complicated. Few people care to think about it: the sexual role you play at any given time is *relative* to many factors. It might well be called *the gay theory of relativity!*

Some observations concerning the gay theory of relativity, which I present for your consideration before you go out cruising tonight:

1. Young gays do not like the role-playing labels; they say correctly that they reserve the right and fun of doing anything with anybody (at almost any time). They call it pansexuality.

Quoted recently in the magazine NEW YORK, one long-haired, sixteen-year-old youth from Long Island explained it this way: "Everywhere you go, everybody looks the same. They're all wearing the same hairdos, the same clothes, the same eight-inch platform shoes, and they're all taking Quaaludes and listening to the same transvestite rock groups. Pretty soon everybody seems to meld together, and any body that feels good is all right." I appreciate that attitude and it does make for living freer and greater experimentation *when you're young*.

The labels, however, did not invent the roles. As one grows older, one begins to observe a certain pattern in one's sexual responses; *more than not*, one discovers and seeks to play either a dominant or submissive part. (Also called active-passive, although a so-called passive role can be active indeed; if you've worked over a trick from toe to scalp with your tongue for hours, then blown him for an hour more, heaven knows that's action, but the role is still the so-called passive one. I told you this was complicated. Other names of the game—none of which fit perfectly—are: butch-fem; giver-receiver; master-slave; sadist-masochist—all much the same in varying degrees of intensity.)

2. Older, and having presumably discovered one's role (more than not), one can still feel sexually stifled and in order to function at all, must go out and play *the opposite role, briefly.*

3. Trouble between young lovers living together develops when the mish-mash joy of just tumbling into bed wears off, and they begin to separate out into their roles and discover they both want to dominate (which leads to fistfights) or they both want to submit (which leads to mutual contempt, that awful moment when lovers become sisters).

4. If by chance, or refusal to face facts, someone does not admit into consciousness the primary role he has been playing and the type of people needed to play it, *that* gay person lacks identity. When a relationship "works" for him he has no idea why; when a relationship ends he is totally at sea, and full of blame.

5. Recognizing your more-than-not role is liberating. This understanding is vital for the conduct of an affair—one is in the position then to make a *willed* choice: "My lover never dominates me and I need it occasionally, but I have a mostly fulfilling relationship with him and I can survive without too much discomfort."

Further observations:

6. If you've always considered yourself a leader in life, it can be horrendous to admit you mostly get expiated (laid) by kneeling before and sucking off some dim-wit and stalwart piece of trade. That's a tough need to recognize in oneself, tougher yet to implement, and damned tough to live with afterward. But if it is the case, and you are to function, all three things must come to pass. (Gay submissive role episodes happen not infrequently with married, ambivalent, but mostly heterosexual human beings. How can such a reversal of roles on the part of her manly husband ever be explained to the wife? If discovered, it must be devastating for an unaware woman.) It is equally devastating to an unaware submissive homosexual partner to discover the very same fact about his ostensibly dominant lover.

Going on if it is possible at all becomes more complicated, but more realistic. One learns to *live with complication, a great secret of existence*; one becomes sophisticated—which means "highly complicated" according to Websters, and "wise" in Greek. Or, because one is unable to accept *the way things are*, the love affair breaks up.

7. A word about the human sexual situation. The facts—known for years by enlightened people—are these: everyone is ambivalent sexually, whether they repress it or not, depending on time, place and the partner at hand. Men and women are (1) both heterosexual and homosexual, but predominantly one or the other, and (2) there is another ambivalence: within each of those orientations one may play a dominating or submissive role, but again, predominantly (I use the term "more-than-not" in this book), one or the other. Think about it, *please*.

8. Ignore or rebel against role-playing, if necessary, as an experiment to get your stuck sex life started again. You may be the exception to the rules, and, excepted, live happily. But for more of us than not, these archetypal gay roles exist—and have ancient beginnings in the human race; they do not exist—as the young are prone to believe—merely because everybody has agreed upon them, like daylight savings time. For the most of us, roles exist, *period*. One ignores their reality, with all its mind-boggling complication, at one's peril.

9. I stress that this is gay *sexual* role-playing. It does *not* necessarily *extend out of bed*. If so (and it is natural and comfortable for both lovers in an affair), fine. But if one or both *force* each other to extend their roles out of bed—trouble. In bed—one way. Out of bed—equals, loving friends, and, yes, gentlemen. (More on this in Chapter 14.)

10. Keep in mind that your more-than-not sexual role will govern to some extent what you wear, and where and how you cruise. It will very much govern *whom* you cruise and whose cruising of you you accept. And it governs almost completely what you do in bed with a specific person. There are, however, some *significant generalities* that can be made—regardless of your role—about clothing, where and how to find a lover for the night (or maybe longer), and how to do best what you do do in bed. All of which adds up to your sensual know-how and aura. All of which is going to make you more devastatingly attractive to HIM!

Perhaps, instead of cruising tonight, you'd prefer to think this over a bit. Are there any questions?

All right, you there, in the violet crushed-velvet.

What role more-than-not do *I* play?

Ah ha!

More-than-not I play . . . no, on second thought that is for me to know and you to find out. But I'll say this: if we ever meet in person and you should ask me, I promise to tell you. I may even show you.

6

DRESSING YOUR BLUES AWAY/LOOKING SEXY FOR HIM

You've been in a blue funk about your sex life; you haven't paid attention, and your wardrobe's gone to hell. Cheer up—the hints and suggestions that I'm going to give you in this chapter about your clothes will have you looking better fast. When you look better, you'll feel better, and you'll be on your way toward possessing and exuding that sensual aura which is going to spider so many into your web (read bed).

Now don't throw up your hands and say, "My God, there's so much to choose from! What look do I want?"

A rich profusion of clothing styles and individual garments does exist. The wet look, the Gatsby look, the soft look, the elegant look, the casual look . . . not to mention safari outfits, matching shirt and pants combinations, wide lapels, narrow belts, flairs or baggies, cuffs or no cuffs, platform shoes, art deco accessories—bewildering!

You're not alone; most people feel bewildered. The only people these days who express certainty about men's fashion are the copywriters who blithely dictate it. They have to seem authoritative or they'd lose their jobs. So to keep them employed the rest of us are kept spinning with new trends every time another issue of a fashion magazine hits the stands. I know—I used to write men's fashion copy. But more important, for ten years—on and off—I sold men's clothing and haberdashery. I think, with that background, I can steer you straight (wisely) about how to dress so that you look good to yourself, and to a prospective bed partner.

Let's start with your jeans. If you've kept your figure or are getting it back with the exercise system, you can wear jeans advantageously right into the mortuary. I know one elderly queen who insisted he be buried in them; his reasoning was correct: he'd lived in them, he might as well die in them. The family acceded to his wishes, I'm told, but the coffin was open for viewing only above his waist: his casket basket existed to please him, went unobserved to please the family.

We have all been infatuated with someone wearing jeans, and it was a toss-up which we were attracted to, the person or—those wonderful, faded-blue, downy-soft, well-worn, splitting-seam, bulging-crotch, packed-ass dungarees. Once, for me it was the jeans: he couldn't understand my perceptible change of attitude when he shed that gorgeous second skin and revealed mere hips and legs. So let us say just that everyone should have several pairs of jeans; ditto Levi cut-offs, and, alas, move on.

Three things to keep in mind when buying clothes:

1. *What the current styles are.*

You find this out two ways. *First*, by poring over the fashion magazines: Esquire, Gentlemen's Quarterly, Playboy, After Dark. Also by looking at some of the better women's magazines to see what the male models are wearing. Also, by looking at the specifically gay magazines: the stuff is usually too much, but that is how taste is developed: by knowing the best and worst example of any particular thing, and all the gradations in between. The *second* way to inform yourself about the better styles is to go to the best men's shops in your area and actually see what is being offered. See it, and try it on. You mustn't feel self-conscious about this; neither you nor the clerk can know in advance what's going to be right for you. You might indeed buy the article in question; at least you'll know what you don't like. I am in favor of lightly cruising department store salesmen; they can be valuable friends when it comes to giving you personal advice on an article, or suggesting a garment, or an accessory that you couldn't have known about. I imagine men's department salesmen never lack for lovers: you should see some of those stores on a Saturday afternoon (many gay people bring their brunch).

2. *What your so-called perennial style is.* This means the colors or fabric or even cut of garment that you know you *always look good in.* Most people are aware of this by the time they're old enough to cruise: if you don't know it, find out by studying yourself in the mirror or asking friends. I mean real friends, not a bitch who'll put a sack on you to eliminate competition or a lover who likes you best bare but happily enjoys any silly frock you choose to wear. What color brings out your eyes? Can you bear strong patterns, or had you best stick to subtle solid colors? Do the newest pinched-cut waist style jackets become you or hourglass your figure disproportionately? Are you the type to don baggies the cuffs of which drag the ground like a wedding dress? Are long-rise pants your dish of tea, or short-rise—remember that short-rise pants are sometimes so tight in the crotch that you'll be able to show a nice basket but never be able to get an erection. Do form-fitted shirts fit you, or ride up on your torso and bunch as badly as, if not worse than, a full-cut shirt? Keeping in mind that even synthetic fabric shrinks a little, do you like and are you able to wear high tight collars or had you best plan to buy shirts with collars that allow you to talk? Are those platform shoes really comfortable for wearing all day at the office or do they ruin your disposition after the first hour? Can you get away with camp clothes or do you look like Abe Lincoln in a Clovis Ruffin caftan? You can by this kind of examination know what to wear, regardless of the current styles.

3. *When you're buying clothes, keep in mind the clothes you*

already own. So-called impulse buying is satisfying to the ego at the moment. But how many times have you bought something that was great-looking in the store and when you got it home looked dreary on you and, morever, dove-tailed with nothing else in your wardrobe? I know gay people with closets full of these oddments. They are perfectly honest when they say they have nothing to wear. Gay people not only enjoy being stylish—they can carry off new styles and even originate them. (I remember Harry and David sporting bell-bottoms in 1964; I thought they might get zapped in the street. We have Los Angeles to thank for much of what we wear informally: the mad, merry lifestyle of Californians delights me.) *The trick to benefiting from new styles is to combine in your wardrobe things that you have with the things that you currently acquire.* Speaking of gay people originating style: did you know that until World War I wrist watches were considered effeminate? Mostly gays wore them. Tomorrow, the world!

Inside Dope Regarding Fit and Rightness

1. *Pants*

A short rise is preferable, but as I said, if it's too short, you'll choke to death. Also, pants should outline your buttocks nicely, not crease in the cleft so that you are defined cheek by cheek. See if the side pockets bulge inordinately, or if the material ripples between the pocket and the fly—if so, too tight. Cuff length is long these days, with a break at the shoe; if they're too long, however, the back of the cuffs will get dirty and frayed pretty fast. Although wide-leg pants are in, be sure there isn't too much the effect of bloomers, especially around the thigh in the back. Alterations won't help—forget that particular pair of pants. About the waist-line: if it is a bit too small and you really do intend to lose weight, buy them; the whole pair of pants will be smaller proportionately than the next size up, and when you lose, they'll look fine. (Have the smaller size pants waist let out temporarily.) My problem has been that I promise myself to lose, then I don't. Once, I had my come-uppance. With my new pair of pants comfortably unzipped, I was driving down Interstate 95 from Boston to New York, going about 60 in the speed lane on a crowded highway. Suddenly, the right rear wheel of my VW Ghia fell off (I learned later); all I felt was a lurch and the car began to zig-zag as I fought the wheel to turn in the direction of the skid—and I prayed that the cars in the other lane, and especially behind me, could get out of the way. My car spun, tires screeching, completely around twice before it came to a halt, thank God upright, and stopped facing oncoming traffic. The woman behind me, in a station wagon, had done an expert piece of driving, zigging when I zagged, avoiding a collision. With what I thought was great presence of mind, I turned off my ignition, snapped on the flicker danger lights, and got out. The station wagon had stopped and the woman put her flicker lights on, too. I courteously saluted her, and with that, my pants fell down.

2. *Coats, sport or suit.*

Yes, the clothing for sale in a store's University Shop is less expensive than in the Men's Department and, yes, you have kept your figure mostly. Mostly. You will, if you're honest, have to admit there have been changes, especially when you try to fit into that University Shop clothing with its narrow armholes and narrow chest patterns (which cause the lapels to bulge instead of roll). Not to mention the shallow pockets and limited choice of materials (generally not strong and definite designs). You may save money, but the coat will not look stylishly pinched, just skimpy. Wherever you buy a jacket, see if the collar hugs your neck properly; if not, don't take a chance. Also see if the jacket when you button it breaks around the middle; if so, too tight, but alteration is possible. Expensive clothes are expensive because they're better tailored, subject to extensive alteration, and keep their shape longer. Good material keeps its nap and color, too. Cheap clothing is cheap because the fabric is poorer, the garment is mass designed, the seams are largely unalterable, or so costly to alter that most stores won't bother. Always better to have one good garment that fits you than two cheapies that don't.

3. Shirts

Shirts are the biggest rip-off in the haberdashery business. Pert and colorful in the store, all done up with pins, sizing in the material (which goes with the first washing), tissue paper and cardboard . . . get them home, wear them, wash them a few times—they fade and become either too small with shrinkage or a shapeless mess so that you wonder if it's the same shirt. Beware shirts in the store with thread-ends hanging from button-holes, and shirts with big buttons: they pop the fastest. As I said before, contour-cut shirts tend to ride upward on your body and end up bunching worse than shirts cut full at the bottom.

4. Ties.

Coordinate ties with shirts; buy them together, if possible, bring the shirts to the tie counter, then take your time gauging what goes with what. Again, there's a difference between a well-made (and expensive) tie and a cheap tie. The well-made one won't slip when you knot it and if it creases in the knot area, those creases will hang out overnight. The opposite is true of the cheap tie. Good ties, good shirts and shoes can offset cheap suits.

5. *Shoes.*

As tough as this news may be on your budget, good shoes are a must of musts. A good shoe will be well-made in order to give your feet *arch support* as well as style. Too many shoes are all style and nothing else—one instance where looks can kill, almost. Those platform shoes that you wear are going to break your feet, as well as your disposition. Foot doctors rub their hands greedily, knowing it won't be long before they have lots of new patients! For you shorties, though, there's nothing wrong with wearing a well-made platform shoe. People judge your character by your shoes more than by any other single item. Keep them always looking new, even if they aren't.

6. *Synthetic Fabric.*

Try always in shirts, suitings, to get cotton or wool mixed in with whatever synthetic element there is in the fabric. It always says somewhere what the fabric is made of. Beware of 100 per cent synthetic anything. It's hot, it doesn't absorb perspiration, and it may cause heat rash. Scientists haven't invented a fabric yet that is *perfectly* wash'-n-wear: a touch-up is always needed after a while.

* * *

Your style is what *you* look good in, what works for *you*. The only way to tell is by trying things on; if you experiment sufficiently—in this area, as in others—you will develop a knack of being able to judge pretty quickly what's for you and what isn't.

Fashion this year, tipping its hat to the '30's, is a return to naturalness and simplicity. Said Bill Blass recently in Esquire: "You get awfully tired of bold clothes. Men have rediscovered, even young men, that you look positively nifty in a navy blue suit. What I want to put across is that there's something equally sexy and attractive about somebody looking like a gent." Esquire tells us to make the blue blazer our wardrobe workhorse, and that the sum-up of fashion feeling now is, "handsome, well-chosen clothes worn with a natural and relaxed air." Which is what I've been telling you. Actually, that's the perennial style of styles.

If I had to define taste in a single word, I'd say "appropriateness." Appropriate to your age, to the occasion, to the part of the country (what's great in N.Y., may bomb in L.A. or Dallas), to the weather and even to the time of day or night. Your job is to blend current fashion, your perennial style, and taste into your own look. When you're dressing seriously.

Joke clothes are another matter. You know—the funky look, when clothes are a costume, not an outfit. I like joke clothes on the right people, invariably the young. West Point Cadet coats, pea jackets, John-boy ("The Waltons") overalls with butterflies and patches sewn on, bullet cartridge belts, boots with turned-down socks, metal studs on everything, ditto rhinestones, six-inch-heel multi-colored platform shoes—any of its adaptable immediately as plumage for a satanic rock group.

With rare exceptions, for kids. On you, if you're over thirty, most probably a turn-off to anyone who can see you even in a bar half-light. You may think you look like a dream; others will think you're dreaming. In trying for an impossible effect, you lose all of the positive effects you *can* create. Over thirty, joke clothing is a joke and it's on you in more ways than one. I admit I saw some joke clothing on Fifth Avenue the other day that moved me: I saw two men wearing full-length mink coats. I liked it fine.

But, you ask, will all this result in my looking sexy?

Yes, absolutely. We have already tacitly agreed that for hard-eyed late-night cruising, nothing is better than your jeans. At any other time, what you look sexy in is the same as what you look attractive in. Believe me, if you follow the hints and suggestions for dress in this chapter, you'll be dynamite as you walk in the bar door. Your aura will shine. I might add that if you've followed the exercises given earlier, your muscle tone and even your skin tone will be improving and both of those have a subtle effect on the way the material of your clothing falls on you.

One clothing problem we gays don't really have (unless your partner is a drag queen, bless etc.) is attire for the bedroom. A pair of jockey shorts will do, or a ratty but clean old terrycloth robe or, best—nothing, just nothing at all!

7

ONE FOR OUR SIDE, OR BE GLAD YOU'RE GAY

You must know heterosexual couples where you live. I know some near me. People your own age, I mean—friends of long standing. Maybe you're invited to dinner once a month, as I am; you bring flowers for the wife and toys for the children. It is an evening of talk about their family, what the two males do for a living, or what the wife has been doing. You care about them and you're convinced that they think of you as an intimate friend. No one, least of all yourself, considers you the family homosexual pet.

If you're like me, the subject of your homosexuality almost never arises. They know it; you have made no attempt to hide it. When there's a gay news event, you bring it into the conversation and everyone has a chuckle. You do not personalize your homosexuality. You realize if you do, no matter how sophisticated they may be—the husband's eyes go glassy, the wife fidgets or has to leave her cocktail to see how dinner is coming.

You may find the new gay lib consciousness will modify those evenings. Here's what happened to me the other night.

The Joneses (let's call them that) have been my friends for over a decade. Dan Jones has done well as a publishing house editor and I enjoy our conversation about literature and he never fails to delight me with current literary chit-chat. Helen, his wife, is a lovely cultured WASP girl of sensitivity, supportive to her husband and—as far as possible—to me. The other night when I went to their place (occasionally I take them out), I was surprised to find them both in a state of agitation. The previous evening (they told me as I sipped my first dry martini), they had been to the theatre to see "Find Your Way Home." I hadn't seen it but I knew that it was a play which dealt super-frankly with homosexuality. I gathered that the performance had made them feel "up" on the subject and that they had decided between them it was something that concerned me and that they'd never made any effort to let me share it with them. Commendable, I thought, and said nothing.

On the second round of drinks, Helen brought the subject again into the conversation and said, "David, you must have a friend you'd like to bring along to dinner. We'd be happy to have him." I nodded appreciatively but was silent.

On the third round of drinks, Dan repeated verbatim what Helen had said (with no apparent lead-in) about bringing a friend. He added that I must feel free with them about my homosexuality: he apologized for his bluntness but said he wanted me to get the message without fail. All right, I thought, this is the moment.

I had, as a matter of fact, recently met someone I liked and, after brief consideration, I told them about him and said I believed they would enjoy his company as well as mine for an evening. Yes, I would bring him next time.

"Where did you meet him?" Helen asked.

"I met him in a bar," I said.

"Oh," she said. "In a bar."

And she got up to see how dinner was coming.

"You're compatible with him . . ." Dan said. "In bed?"

"Yes," I said. "He's very good in bed."

With my remark, their three-year-old child entered the room, sat quietly on the floor at my feet. Helen returned, and I continued on a bit about my new friend, his job, his looks, his personality. Helen jumped up and swooped the 'child into her arms.

"I'll just put Jamie to bed," she said, and—with the child held forward like a crucifix proferred to foil the onslaught of Dracula—she departed.

At dinner, which was served by their maid, once again they brought up the subject of my friend. "But are *you* really satisfied?" Dan asked. They were certainly trying hard, I thought, and out of respect, I must answer. I did so in specific but not vulgar detail. As I spoke, I noticed that Dan colored, and his head seemed to hunker down between his shoulders. Helen fidgeted with food on her plate. I offered a further innocuous remark about homosexuality and Dan said, "I think that can wait until after dinner." Fine with me: we spoke of Jackie and Ari.

After dinner and after two brandies and a scotch, which is our custom together, Helen suddenly broke.

"David," she said, "please understand. I care about you . . ."

"And I about you both," I interjected.

"But there's something about the whole subject . . . of homosexuality that gets me. I think I comprehend it abstractly," she said. "But the reality of it . . . especially the lingo . . . gay, suck, anus, oral penetration . . . oh, I know all those words . . . but somehow it seems that every word about it is concerned and focused on sexuality *down there* . . . penis . . . analingus . . . testes . . ." Head bowed, she trailed off.

I genuinely shared with her a sense of discomfort, and realized how it must sound to them—unavoidable words if the subject was to be discussed—but from their point-of-view, awful.

"Yes," Dan added. "Somehow to us the necessary words are offensive. Not your fault . . . can't blame anybody . . . Just the fact about it, the verbal pictorial conceptions, words.''

I left them at eleven, as I usually do; we parted as always, cordially, and Helen, as is our custom, said she would call me about the day of our dinner-date next month. Nor was she careless: she plainly reiterated their invitation to my friend.

Going home on foot (my place is only a few blocks from theirs and I still like to walk at night in New York), I shared again their feeling about the words necessary to describe homosexuality even perfunctorily.

Then I got to thinking about the problems of homosexuality and living in the world as an overt homosexual. It occurred to me that, in spite of all, the ecstasies of gay life outweighed the drawbacks, words or no words. Conscious of words, I began to think of things *in, on, or about one's partner in gay life that one does not have to contend with*, and the words that describe them.

We, as gay people, do *not* have to contend with bloody menstrual periods, opening car doors, fingering the clitoris, protecting the honor of a partner from gossip, picking partners up at home and returning them necessarily, virginity, pregnancy, diaphragms, condoms, black or white gloves one of which is forgotten and for which one must go back, frigidity, lacy nighties, vaginas, vaginal jellies, dried-up vaginal fluids, Femiron pills, vaginal deodorizers, the big pill, peignoirs in pink silk, daily hat compliments, breasts (pendulous or small), breast ulcers, the belief that the world revolves around the vagina, hair curlers, fingernails painted or chipped, smudged lipstick, surprise at anal sex, false eyelashes, lighting cigarettes, holding chairs at table, rising when a partner enters the room, holding doors, paying for every damn thing, black stockings secured by garters, allowing a partner precedence through a door, marriage contracts and divorce settlements, alimony, babies that screech in the night, breastfeeding, little black dresses, puckering skirts, runs in stockings, panty hose, beauty salons, gynecologists, references to the vagina et al as ''plumbing'' (ugh), droopy hems, tampons, boudoirs, pussy, little print sun dresses, cunt, toplessness, ornate hair styles, wide hips and wide-hipped slacks, adultery, introducing one's partner as Ms., remembering to put down toilet seats, cunnilingus, and lovely hands.

Don't get me wrong. I have regard and respect for women, and many women friends whose company I enjoy and cherish. I want you to like women; as I've said. But gay people—count your blessings!

8

FIGHT AGAINST GAY FEARS

Please stand in front of a mirror. Observe closely. Your hair
has body and natural sheen. Your face is fresh and clear; your
eyes are bright. Your clothing: it's right for you and in tune with
the times. You've been following the hints and suggestions I've
offered about grooming and dress—you've performed your sensitivity and physical exercises (Chapter 2) faithfully. The
outward you is shaping up; there's a real glow: your sensual aura,
of course. You are rapidly on your way to becoming a full sensuous homosexual human being.

In the next several chapters, we're going to concentrate on the
inner elements, which are also necessary to the total composition
of your aura: evolving your mana (giving) personality, sharpen-
ing your erotic awareness and—in this chapter—fighting fears.

Still at the mirror? Good. You cannot help but conclude that
you look like a person who values his life, who cares about
himself. When a prospective bed partner sees that you do care,
it's an impetus for him to care about you, too. Come away from
the mirror.

Sit down, get comfortable, and contemplate the following: you work—or one way or another—provide for yourself. You keep your word as best you can; you are a responsible man. You can be charming and entertaining when you want to be. And you have a lot to give others—oh, yes you have, you've proven it often. When we're in a down mood (such as you've been in for so long), memory of our generous actions goes out of our minds. Think hard—and you will recall your generous actions (many that others never knew about)—and the scale of balance in regard to your own self-esteem will begin to tip back in your favor (where it should be).

Judging by the *stuckness* of your life, especially your sex life—up until now your relationship with yourself has been out of synch—not bad, but a stand-off between you and you. You haven't liked yourself, you've been your own best friend *hardly at all*.

Let's both identify and personify (for the sake of retaliating) the true enemy. *Fear* is his awful name! And he's a skulking bastard, he gets in where you least expect him, and his efforts against you can be ruinous. What he can't stand, what destroys him, is your frank admission that he exists, and your frank facing him down. Yes, you've been afraid. Fear has brought you to this state of semi-paralysis—nameless generalized fear. And you know what?—you were right to be afraid; there's plenty to be afraid of in the world. What you *didn't do* was recognize fear; what you *forgot* is that everybody, including me, is scared stiff half the time. What you *haven't known* is how to handle that fear—how to embrace it, live your life constructively in spite of it, make it the spur that drives you!

So let's itemize and confront and dispose of fears that you, as a gay person expecially, are susceptible to:

Fear of exposure. Maybe the A Number One bug-a-boo. All right, suppose some straight person you know well did catch you in a compromising situation—entering or leaving a notorious gay bar. And suppose he's the type to get righteously indignant.

Do you press the panic button?

Not if you're making progress as a sensuous homosexual human being, you don't. You're learning to live your own life. If that particular straight person is offended—that's his problem. Your legitimate concern now is truly to do your own thing, especially in regard to sex, and without guilt. Loyal to yourself, you're in the right; you're working with the physical, emotional and mental equipment you were born with—you're doing your best. Those offended straight dummies are rapidly being left and lost by the wayside.

Which is not to say that you should buy a red magic marker and paint a big H or G on your chest then streak provocatively through public places.

What do I care if people stare
Or care what people say?
For the golden dogs I'm going to
Are handsome dogs and gay!

Charming as a four-liner verse, but not at all adequate as a life precept, though fun to contemplate.

Your position in life as a human being who happens to be gay is curiously similar to the position in life of human beings who happen to be super-rich. The super-rich bear their stewardship of immense financial resource. You, as a gay person, bear a stewardship of "an aristocracy of the sensitive, the considerate and the plucky"—as E. M. Forster wrote in an allusion to gays. Both stewardships are special. When there is something special about you, people who are not special sense it; it frightens them, and they try to bring it down.

According to friends of mine who are articulate and also possessors of great wealth (a rare combination), it's tough and estranging to live with what they have. They say they feel paranoid—even though they know it may not be justified—about others' motives regarding themselves.

Similarly, it is tough to live in our society with knowledge of oneself as a homosexual. Inevitable paranoia! (Sometimes justified, sometimes not.) At the very least—in a world almost totally oriented to heterosexuality—a gay person is locked into an existence of irony and contradiction.

You and I, as gay people, and the super-rich, are burdened then with marvelous-awesome stewardships that require levelheadedness—and the ability, as I've said (and say again for emphasis), of *handling complication*. You are learning to manage that, with the taste and perspective you're acquiring in this book.

O.K., great, you say—but suppose my parents or my bigoted boss find out I'm gay?

Dear friend, it's happened to me and to many others that I know. Guess what: I assure you from vivid personal experience and the recounted experiences of my friends that nowadays, absolutely everybody involved in the incident—yourself included—*survives*. You and your human relationships enter an entirely new Phase. You discover that you can get along great without the people who refuse to acknowledge the validity of your existence. Really! Hard to believe, I know; but it's true—it's the way the thing works out. Of course you suffer. And then you grow up. And you are in command of yourself far more firmly than before; you are a person, an individual with a hardwon and conscious identity. Those gay people who do not go through such an experience may lose forever their chance of becoming somebody. When the cat's out of the bag, the cat is invariably better for it.

Fear of Competition in the World. I am saddened by the number of my gay friends who are not only stuck in their sex lives but stuck in their *careers*. Overburdened by guilt about being gay—distracted, even fragmented by it—they do not utilize one quarter of the stuff that's in them. Wanting love and to be relieved of oppression, they sacrifice any real talent they possess for *peace*. They hold routine jobs, live in tiny apartments, engage in desultory affairs, make do with a small circle of friends. It is a high price to pay for peace, and their situations become bitter as time goes on. It's as if, existing that way, they felt they could hang on to their tattered rag of self-respect. Later on, they'll be sorry that they didn't strike out in the world—that they succumbed to fear:

I worked for a menial's hire,
  Only to find, dismayed,
That any wage I'd asked of life
  Life would have paid.

If the narrowing circle of experience I have described seems to be what is happening in your life, *here's what to do*: have the courage to go back through doors that seemed closed, either by others or by yourself, and *rethink your career situation*. Young or old, no matter what you've been doing—you possess a unique talent, ability or aptitude. You must discover it or even re-discover it. For better or worse, we live in a world that operates on the barter system. It will reward you with cash, recognition and self-esteem for whatever talent, ability or aptitude you can offer it. And if you do not offer it anything unique in the way of a dream, the price you pay is to be caught up and made useful in someone else's dream.

Inner tension? Yes, that's the problem. First, realize that the tension incurred in you by involvement will be far less than you imagine. And, second, realize that as your self-esteem builds on what you have accomplished, fear of the world will diminish proportionately.

Don't let fear of competition stop you for one second! A gay person's contribution to the world's work is as valid as any other's. Often more so, since—once organized—gay people can bring to the struggle elements of their specialness which they have transmuted into talent. Yes, in the process of competitive survival you are vulnerable to exposure and ridicule, subtle or direct. Perhaps even beyond your fair share. So what?! You're learning to be resilient enough to take it; your hide will toughen. Again, you will *survive!*

Whenever I'm in a competitive situation where I find I must put my life on the line to survive, a speech from an old play comes back to me. It reassures me; I hope it will affect you the same way. The speech is from a melodrama of the 1920's (no dear, I didn't see the play, I read it), called *The Shanghai Gesture* by John Colton. It is spoken by a character in the play called Mother Goddam, and she is the owner of the largest brothel in Shanghai. In her speech, she describes how as a gently reared young girl she was sold to the sinister "junk men" operators of floating houses of prostitution. I am told the actress who played the part rendered the following lines in a gutteral voice, rising rapidly in fierce crescendo:

"Yes—yes—yes—all—all I survived—whippings with hippo hide when I was stubborn—hot dung thrust into my nostrils and stinging leeches in my ears so I could not sleep—and I survived!—sulphur burned on my naked back to make my tired body gay . . . soles of my feet cut open and pebbles sewn inside so I could not run away—I survived! I survived it all! Hate helped me—black gods helped me—hell and the devil helped me—I lived! I lived!"

I *have* survived—and so, too, will *you* survive!

If you're really at a loss for your unique possibilities:

1. Go take a *battery of aptitude tests.* A mechanical method of procedure, perhaps, but it works to the extent that it will provide you with a general direction.

2. Ask yourself what you *enjoy doing,* think through how to turn it to your career advantage. And don't overlook what, at first glance, might seem a preposterous avenue of expression.

A friend of mine was trying to get his doctorate in history; he hated the work and the history teaching career that inevitably would follow. His family wanted it for him. What he enjoyed doing was sewing little black dresses. His lover took one of the dresses to a manufacturer and—you guessed it—today, separated from his family but mystically fulfilled, he is one of the country's foremost dress designers.

Another friend, middle-aged, had carved out for himself a mediocre but profitable career in advertising; the only things he liked about his job were the long eating and drinking lunches. Yes, he quit advertising. Today he sits in the Caribbean sun, host at his own restaurant, a drink in one hand, a fork in the other.

And one last example: a friend with great mathematical ability was employed by the government in esoteric technical research. During his dull periods, he doodled on a pad. A fellow researcher saw one of the doodles and commented that the designs were extraordinary. My friend took the pad home, used the doodles as a basis for an abstract painting—yes, he exhibits today in a Fifty-Seventh Street gallery and he's happy for the first time in years.

This sort of thing can happen to you.

Start re-thinking today!

Other fears—particular to gay people:

Fear of Growing Old. When one is young and gay, anybody over the age of thirty seems to inhabit a different world. Thirty seems like the boundary line between disaster and everything you hold dear. But oh my foes and oh my friends (provided you've done something with your life), the love affairs you'll have over thirty, even over forty and fifty! can be graceful, sexy and enduring! *First*, with regular exercise, the body need not go to flab; it can look as toned as it ever looked. If you do keep fit—sex never dies! *Second*, as you pick up on psychological development (with this book), you will retain a young-feeling, young-acting personality; you'll probably reach out on your death bed and try to make the doctor. *Third*, if you become wise on the subject of eroticism—a sensuous homosexual human being—you'll have more lovers hanging around than you can handle. Because, older, you can play a dominant role-with-caring that you simply could not play at an earlier age—you weren't equipped! Or a submissive role-with-understanding—understanding which you do actually possess through experience. Think of the older men you know who score marvelously. Their success (which you may not have conjured) lies in what I am talking about here. As an older person who has coped with life and not been daunted, you have far more to give a lover than you had in youth—and your prospective bed partners are going to sense it.

Fear of Falling in Love. The most awful, grief-stricken experiences in my life have been suffered through as a result of loving someone. At different times and in differing degrees, I have: lost my public respectability, lost my sense of personal identity, lost a good deal of whatever money I had. (One lover even deprived me of future income by chucking a half-finished manuscript of mine into the ocean.) If I had the chance would I do it all over? You bet I would! Am I cautious about falling in love again? Not for a second!

I pity those gays who feel they've been burned and decide never—never! What cloistered hygienic hearts they must possess, what drier-than-dust lives! No sadder people exist than those who are constantly on guard against emotional entanglements. Somerset Maugham commented on this when he said that the tragedy of life is not that men die, but that living, they cease to love.

And if, having been burned, you fall in love and it's hello sucker April Fool again—so what? The most exalting experience known to man is being in love. What you remember later on is not that apartment you kept so absurdly neat, but the wonderful/terrible disheveled times you were bowled over in love. To have been in love a lot is to have participated grandly in the primary business of being alive.

Only the inner satisfaction with one's work in the world runs a far-behind second to the satisfaction of having loved and having been loved in return.

If you claim you've been through the glass-mirrored, funhouse process of love and it's brought you little joy, I say you've simply *forgotten* when you're *just* in love how the days became mud-luscious, puddle-wonderful spring-time days even if it was in the middle of winter!

What can compare with that first kiss between new-found lovers—its serenity, certainty and surrender! No difference if you meet him in a classroom or a barroom. Some say that where you meet presages where you'll both go back to when it's over. Nonsense. The major consideration is that you do meet and that *you have a friend* . . . I can think of few more ecstatic moments in life than when you first really believe that *you have a friend*. The world turns young no matter how old you are—and your five senses throb with receptivity. At the very instant of falling in love, it's as if you heard a trumpet sound,

> . . . *from the hid battlements of eternity*
> *Those shaken mists a space unsettle then,*
> *Round the half-glimpsed turrets slowly wash again.*

Oh, I understand how difficult it is to make room in one's orderly existence for a new lover. Your inflexible but safe routines are disrupted, the look of your prim, shiny life is smudged. The toothpaste he leaves untopped, the shoes of his that you trip over in the dark, the dishes he used and then left unwashed, his laundry piled up in the closet. I know. Take each of those items as evidence that he exists, he's yours and you're his and thank God for the both of you!

Fear of Impotence. Yes, there may be times when you have trouble keeping it up or can't get it up at all.

1. Be sure you're in bed with someone you are sexually attracted to. Gay people often get maneuvered or maneuver themselves into bed situations which seem promising beforehand but are disastrous in realization. You may discover that you both are

uncompromising in your need to play roles and that you both want to play the same role—stymied. Or you've allowed yourself to be lured into bed as a favor, or because you were drunk or because you wanted a favor from the individual and it wasn't sex. Any of these can result in impotence. It does not mean that your sex life is over: it does mean that you are not responding to this particular partner.

2. If you are impotent with someone you are certain that you do like sexually . . . *First*, be sure that fatique or over-indulgence is not inhibiting you. *Second*, stop being so dead-pan earnest about sex, feeling that you have to top your own previous performance or that you're in competition with some guy not present. Learn to kid around with your sexual partner, so that the moment is lightened. *Third*, relax your insistence upon playing your role or upon having him play his. This once, turnabout. Or if you've insisted on mutuality (which is as binding on both lovers as any other role), try submissive-dominant sex: in that regard, no matter your role, learn to hate a little the person you love a lot. Your love-making has become too syrupy sweet, cloying and offering no challenge. If penetrating him or being penetrated by him is heaven to you, be violent—for the kingdom of heaven is achieved by violence, not by aimiable aspiration! Grab him and let both of you be ruffled briefly—let yourself go in terms of sexy language, and encourage him to do the same. You'll find impo-tence flies out the window and sperm flies through the air—if you both learn to tolerate a *creative margin of hostility* between you. In bed and out of bed, too. And it is also a constructive attitude toward other people.

Fear of Premature Ejaculation. Have it, stick around for awhile, try again. It'll be slower the second time, and the third time etc.

Fear of Mental Trouble. If you really feel you're losing your grip—unavailing productivity, shattered concentration, ridden by insatiable and dangerous desires, physically aggressive toward others—arrange to see a psychotherapist. Scrimp, save to pay for it. He can reclaim your life. Often, people don't go when they should, because they have half a conviction that they're beyond help in the sense that their problem has never before been encountered. What a curious pride! The human race has existed yea many thousands of years; every problem has been encountered—most psychological problems that you are sane enough to articulate have answers. Or, if not a flat-out answer, the psychotherapist can start you on a line of inquiry, both intellectual and emotional, that will help you find your own answers. The real difficulty for a person who feels he needs help is locating the right therapist. Every city has a free clinic or two, or a doctor in residence who can steer you to a private therapist with proper credentials. You certainly don't need one whose main concern is to change your sexuality—unless *you* want to. If you have been married for years, then discover that you're gay, you have a problem also best dealt with by a therapist; handling it yourself can be needlessly painful to both you and your wife. A letter or a phone call to the gay-oriented Institute for Human Identity in New York might be the best idea.

You're not losing your grip if you have an occasional mild depression. Just as your body signals its need for a rest by tiring, your mind signals a similar need by depression. Being depressed and relatively unresponsive is the mind's way of recouping energy for its next surge forward. So when you're depressed, utilize your time with quiet concerns and, too, you might give a little thought to what the irreconcilable opposites were in the situation which caused your mind to back off. Even if you can't foresee any solution, it helps hasten your mind's renewed ability to cope to know what caused the depression.

Fear of Rejection. One rejection of yourself by a number does not make you a pariah. Go try the other side of the bar.

Fear of Losing Your Lover. I will cover this in Chapter 14. For now, let me warn you to watch out that you yourself are not unconsciously thrusting your lover into competitive situations to test his love for you, or to prove to yourself how great you are to have someone everybody else is after.

Fear of Women. I've never met a gay person who feared each and every woman he encountered. I have met some gays who disliked individual women as ''trick stealers.'' And a few gays who avoided particular women because they felt—in several justifiable instances that I know of—that the particular women demanded obsequious attention and agreement with every remark. Most homosexuals, I believe, are prone to like women who are in the least supportive (or to whom they can be supportive in such matters as hair, clothes, interior design, etc.). Are prone to like women very much who can conceive their preference sexually. Not the smallest group of gays who like women are the hippie homosexuals for whom the fat little girl is a fixture in their crowd. I like women. I hope you do too. It may be that gay people who, in fact, hopelessly idolize women, are secretly afraid of them. In which case their dreams are haunted by Bette Davis, Tallulah Bankhead, Mae West, Joan Crawford, Liz Burton, Dietrich, Hepburn and others. How perfectly delightful!

*　　*　　*　　*

So—fear. Admit he exists, face him down and poof! he disappears. Yes, it is more difficult than that, but that surely is the way to go. DON'T BE AFRAID—be a person who needs people, as Barbra Streisand used to tell us—reach out, explore, experiment, involve yourself to the point even of vulnerability. Telling you DON'T BE AFRAID is an unsophisticated expeditious homilie, true. But one we need to hear every so often. Be a lover. Of others, of yourself. Lovers are never losers and—DON'T BE AFRAID!

9

YOUR GAY MANA (GIVING) PERSONALITY

I want to show you a *new* way of thinking about yourself, and about your sex life, that will enhance your enjoyment. It may even improve your sexual performance.

It is the concept of *mana*.

Hang in here with me. This chapter's a trip.

Have you ever had a day when everything went absolutely right?

Say you woke up refreshed before the alarm rang. The tie you picked first off the rack went perfectly with the shirt and suit you wanted to wear. The conveyance you took to work wasn't crowded. The gang at work greeted you as if it was your birthday. The ten o'clock coffee wagon arrived on time. Your boss complimented you on a hard report you'd done. That guy in accounting you'd looked over a few times looked back at you and you'd made a lunch date. The lunch went incredibly—good cocktails, good food, great background music, reasonable check, which he'd insisted on sharing—and you'd made a date for that evening! After lunch the afternoon flew by and ended with your boss calling you and saying he'd put you up for a raise. Back home you'd rested and dressed with time to spare so you did the drunken old lady next door a favor and went and got her a bottle as she requested. You feel as if nothing, in fact, would be too much trouble. A friend calls and asks you for fifty and you put an extra twenty in the envelope because you know he needs it and you love him. The guy from accounting arrives punctually at the appointed place; the evening moves with pace and flow: your voice remains subdued, discerning and humorful. After dinner, without a word, he accompanies you home and into bed and your sex together is beautiful and you agree to meet again tomorrow.

A great day, indeed. A day when it might be said that *you had mana*.

Have you ever had a day when everything went absolutely wrong?

Late for work, enemies at every turn in the office, no coffee wagon until almost lunch-time. A serious error discovered in your work that will take days to rectify. God awful food in the company lunchroom, vaguely ill from it through an afternoon with no end. So acid, a blotch appears on your nose. The boss waiting near the elevator to check on who leaves early and you're the first one out. Home late, forgot the key, hang around the cold hallway until the super gets back. Inside, the cat is impatient for its dinner and has clawed the shit out of the curtains. And you're out of cat food. You're so sickish your own dinner tastes terrible. The guy to whom you lent the fifty plus twenty calls to say he's got a job in Hawaii, he'll be in touch. One damn calamity after another. You decide to hell with everything, you'll go to a gay bar and maybe pick someone up. Arriving, you get the half-shoulder brush-off. You go home alone, and can't sleep.

A grim day. A day when it might be said that *you did not have mana*.

Have you ever known someone over a period of time for whom everything seemed to go right?

He gets the call from the Broadway producer and is given the part. The play's a hit and he rents a small new place and gets a Chevy. The movies buy the play and he's asked to do his stage role in the film. He goes to Hollywood, returns, rents a bigger place and gets a Cadillac. He has his clothes tailor-made, begins to know everybody who's anybody in New York, or around the country, for he travels greatly now. During all of this he remains a good lover-friend and you like to be around him. You feel better, indeed, around him—even though he's away a lot—than you do around almost anybody. A suspicion enters your mind that if you stick with him maybe some of his good luck will rub off on you. It does, inasmuch as he calls someone for you whom you would like to influence about your career, and it works. And you get an apartment in his old building because he's put in a good word for you. And then, despite his many engagements, he finds time to help you move and afterwards, knowing you're tired (as he must be), he invites you for dinner. You go to bed with him happily.

It might be said that *your friend had mana and that he transferred some of it* to you.

Have you, on the other hand, ever been friends with someone over a period of time for whom nothing went right?

His flower shop is losing money, he hates being there all day. His lover is on the point of leaving him. He confides in you that he's drunk half the time, which is the only way he can cope. He stays on and off at your place because his lover has moved out and taken their bed. His job-seeking efforts seem to bog down in endless interviews. He gets on the phone to you at work and insists upon relating every detail of his latest calamity. His clothes get sloppy. He comes over every night for liquor and dinner and monologues you incessantly. His self-pity grates on you but you feel sorry for him; you're the only friend he apparently has and you've got to continue to prop him up until he gets hold—which strikes you as a good friend's duty. He does seem stronger after he's talked it out with you.

It might be said that *you had mana and that you transferred it* to him.

Are you beginning to get a feeling for mana?

It is a kind of "giving strength."

Mana is a Polynesian word meaning "the power of the elemental forces of nature embodied . . . in a person."

It has come to mean a person with an unusually potent personality, a giver, even one who is able to heal. In that sense, mana, strength, is transferable.

You or I can have mana. The variest hustler or the swishyest queen can have mana; mana exists in people regardless of and quite apart from their physical circumstances.

Now I am not going to take you on this heavy trip much further. So stay close.

Mana is found, I think, especially in people who attract us sexually; it even may be the very thing that attracts us. Other people find mana in you of the special sort that attracts them. What is mana for you may not be mana for someone else, and vice versa.

If during sex one believes that one is extracting mana, as well as sperm, from one's partner, the experience is heightened. If one believes that, like a God, one is giving mana, as well as one's sperm, to one's partner, the experience is heightened. Mana then becomes *a transferable psychic discharge* and giving it and receiving it, both necessary, *add to the enjoyment of intercourse*, no matter what role you play.

We have been told that sexual satisfaction is largely mental. I agree—the mana concept provides a new kind of mental stimulus for you to add to the range of your sexual delectation.

Mana, as you've probably concluded, is partly a gift of the moment, and partly a matter of your being consciously in touch with your creative unconscious mind. If you'd like to know more about this, read the work of Carl Jung. All you need to know, however, about the giving and getting of mana, has now been told.

Try the mana concept the next time you have sex.

More about mana in action later.

10

HOW TO MEET A FRIEND FOR THE EVENING (AND MAYBE LONGER): CRUISING!

You're eager to go cruising, I know, and put to work what you've learned in this book so far. Therefore, at the end of this chapter, even though we haven't gotten to erotic awareness and sexual technique, I'll send you on the town for a dry run.

I distinguish *three* major categories of cruising technique. But first . . .

Please keep in mind what you've learned about exercise, tactile sensitivity awareness, grooming, dress, the gay theory of relativity and the mana concept: elements of your sensual aura. All must be brought to bear in the process of successful cruising.

All must be brought to bear to put you in the right mood—*poised for fun*. Which means a little smile playing around your lips instead of that strained expression you've usually worn. Remember, as you go out the door—*POISED FOR FUN!*

1. *Eyeball-to-Eyeball Contact or, Your Eyes Have Told Me So*
Most of us are pretty good at this so I'm not going to dwell on it very much. For eyeball cruising you have to be in a great mood, poised for fun and big with lust. *If ever your aura must surround*

you, it's when you cruise eye to eye. The person you're following down the street has got to get your vibes, and you have got to project those vibes. Because this eyeball method is practically wordless. The only conversation you may have with him is agreeing whether it will be his place or yours. These instantly formed alliances in life seem to imitate art—especially film art. Gay people really do pick up on one another just by a consenting and appreciative glance. It's romantic; it happens frequently. So, keep that aura of yours burnished bright; you can never predict when it may be required for urgent communication.

2. *Cruising Butches*

What I have to say here will appeal to a minority group of readers. But they are a strong minority, and you may find yourself among them at one period or another of your life. Further, they are a close-mouthed group about the specifics of their procedures, and jealous of interlopers. For that reason, and because I want to save you from a black eye or broken teeth, I'm going to tell all I know.

Part of my knowledge about the subject I gleaned from a dear friend, let's call him Henry. Henry is forty, he has an open face, a frank manner and a small private income which allows him free time to devote to his art: cruising butches. With Henry, it is a high art. He is devoted. So much so, that if you're a friend of Henry's and invite him to dinner, first, don't expect him at all; second, don't expect him on time. Because if Henry spies a desirable butch from his car window, everything else must be put aside for the pursuit and conquest of the butch. I have known of instances where Henry drove around and around the same block for an hour because some butch was leaning up against a telephone pole. Or, if Henry is on foot, I have known him to walk up and down the street past a restaurant window for an hour because a butch was inside having coffee. Ditto a butch on a park bench.

Not just any butch appeals to Henry. Square jaw, thick neck, bulging biceps, thighs curved like a cobra's hood, hands like hams—all this is a necessity for Henry. But I have seen him cruise almost to the point of conquest several specimens of the type—then snap his fingers and walk away (Henry and I used to cruise a lot together). Why did he do it? Walk away, I mean. "Not really me," Henry says. He means that although one butch may resemble every other butch *to me*, only that *special butch* has *mana* for Henry.

Let us follow Henry through the organized and specific steps of his butch-cruising procedure after he has spotted a butch he really wants. It's a lesson for us all.

Say it is the one Henry spied in the restaurant having coffee. The first mistake an amateur might make is to go charging up to the well-lit counter and force a seat next to the quarry. Henry? Never. Henry waits until the butch finishes his coffee, comes strolling out, and ambles down the street, signaling to Henry that the butch really is putting himself on the line. Henry follows —walks fifty feet behind, imitates the way the butch carries himself—what he does with his arms, how he swings his whole body. This is to get into the butch's mood so that when they talk, finally, Henry'll automatically be on the butch's level. Also, it's sexy.

The butch sits on an empty bus-stop bench near the corner. Does Henry rush over? Not on your life; he stops at the corner as if enjoying a breath of air and he lights a cigarette with exaggerated slowness. Naturally the butch inspects him; Henry gives the butch this chance because if the butch does not like what he sees it is the last opportunity he's going to have to move along. In our scene, the butch maintains his position and Henry has scored his first point.

Pretending to indulge a fleeting whim, Henry also sits on the bench and breathes a long exhale of smoke as if to say what a pleasant small-town thing to do—take a little air and your ease on a bench along the main street. Henry lets a minute or two go by—he also lets a bus come and go from the stop and of course the butch doesn't move a muscle. "Oh, those muscles!" Henry is thinking as he looks at them out of the corner of his eye—Henry's eyes have much-used corners: never knew a gay who could do a barroom sweep and tell you who was there and whether there was anyone for him—the way Henry could. O.K. coming up to step two. I hope you're taking notes.

His voice pitched three octaves below its normal range, and at the same time mashing out his cigarette in a manly fashion with his heel, Henry says, "Not much to do in this town, is there?" Everything rides on whether or not the butch responds. Henry waits for a second, two—heaves a sigh of relief as the butch says no, there isn't.

This juncture is easy. The idea is to make shorter and shorter statements while the butch's statements get longer and longer. The conversation's orchestration is rigid and obvious to everyone except the poor butch.

Sure as hell, the butch opens up about himself, and a butch's remarks on his own life are always dynamite. Half of most gay writers' material comes from fantastic-minded butches such as we have under observation here. The stories are marvelously varied but always with some points in common. The butch's family is rich but the butch doesn't get along with his father so he bowed out years ago. The butch has a big business in the middle west that runs itself while he's away. He has a girl waiting to marry him, and a Cadillac in storage. He's in this town to start a business that'll make him rich. "What business?" Henry asks. Selling fresh orange juice to the restaurants each morning: he'll go around himself on a bicycle. "Ah!" Henry answers in an awed tone, and suggests a walk down the street in the direction of the neon lights and people—and the bars. Walking, Henry asks to be told more. The butch regales him with maudlin love epics, and the point of each is that some girl pursued him to her distraction while he couldn't care less about any of them. He has been on the march toward . . . he does not or cannot say . . . his soul—but he makes it clear that that would have been his poetic expression.

It is drink time. Henry never rushes a butch to his pad. There is still preliminary probing to do. After the first drink, which Henry buys (the butch saying that he just arrived and he's a little short), the conversation gets around to queers. Another tense moment for Henry. If the butch says he wants to smash their faces every time he sees one and he's seen plenty, Henry spies a friend on the other side of the bar and goes over and ostensibly forgets the butch. If, however, the butch says his motto is live and let live, Henry orders another round of beers. Amateurs might be tempted at the bar to order their favorite drink, a pink lady or a black russian or a daiquiri, but you don't if you want to maintain your butch front. All right, the butch reiterates that if the queers don't bother him, he doesn't bother them. A good sign—you (Henry in this instance) are going to score. Incidently, if the butch is out-rightly hostile, Henry lets him cool, maybe several days, maybe a week or more: the courting period is lengthened, that's all. Henry will get him.

Henry takes the third step. He picks out some tiny detail from whatever the butch has said, and supports the opposite point of view. Butches, Henry knows, love to argue. They get their stran-gulated vocal chords from arguing and yelling at home in the tenement. Henry builds an argument, knock-down, drag-out—almost. Henry knows how to start and stop the butch's flow by a smile, a wink, a comradely clap on the back (meanwhile cares-sing the lat muscles). Henry can guide the butch to the brink of a fight, gracefully give in, back-track until the butch becomes more and more subdued.

Henry has a medieval mind with theological overtones. Theologians in the Middle Ages prided themselves, I understand, on their ability at disputation. (Didn't they argue about how many angels could stand on the head of a pin?) Realities weren't important, just the ability to one-up your opponent until he gave in. Henry to a T.

The butch is subdued but Henry is still arguing, buying beers, throwing his arms and legs and torso around in the manner of an enthusiastic debater. The butch, meanwhile, is swaying unsteadily on his bar stool, silent, his excess energy quite drained.

This is the sign that Henry has been waiting for—he stops arguing. Blearily (after eight beers), the butch blinks his eyes and says, "Hey, man . . . you're a fuckin' good talker . . . I like you . . . you're my buddy . . . here's to you, man." And the butch toasts his own imminent downfall, with beer.

The next step is home and shortly to bed. "It's getting late," Henry says. "Whyn't we go to my place, I got some beer." Great, man, says the butch, exhausted, really wanting just to sack out. But Henry steers the dear, wobbling, delicious mass of juicy flesh gently along to his place. More beer, a little pot, a final flurry of argument, from which the butch pointedly retreats. Then Henry turns on the TV late movie, joins the butch on the couch. The butch's beer can is slipping from his hand, the vast shoulders are humped and slowly falling over in Henry's direction and whammo! Henry grips the prize and he's home free!

It takes effort, but Henry claims it's worth it.

Oh yes, the art form of cruising butches has one final step. In the morning, Henry is subject from the butch to the "geez-was-I-drunk-last-night" routine. To belie it, and score a final ringing victory, Henry persists and does the butch again right there and then. The butch leaves a hulking shell of his former self.

Henry's butch-cruising technique is, in my estimation, the archetypal form. And, having been exposed to it here, you—and I, to be sure—can learn from it what to do and do it correctly as well as what not to do and save ourselves a nasty bruise.

3. The third major category of cruising technique is the one where most of us fit. *Simple, honest, everyday approaches to*

whomever looks good to you.

The crucial factors in this category are proximity to the gay you want, and wisdom and smoothness in your delivery of that first line, that all-important first line. Muttering, stuttering, stammering or otherwise faultily executing the first line can *spell disaster*. *An irrelevant* first line is not to be thought of.

Here are briefly noted some likely *cruising grounds* and some suggested *first liners.* If you use them, I'll be delighted; if they stimulate you to come up with some of your own, that is even better. Each one presumes that you *have* gained near proximity to the desired trick. And that you must speak first.

AT THE SUPERMARKET:
"Will the price of these frogs' legs never go down?"

AT THE YMCA:
"I adore weight lifters. Can you curl a hundred?"

AT THE CURB ON YOUR STREET:
"Dogs are such a comfort."

ANYTIME, ANYWHERE:
"Got a match?"

AT THE CAR WASH:
"How amazing, all those little brushes!"

AT THE GAY ORGANIZATION PSYCHOLOGICAL BULL SESSION:
"After I masturbated my father . . ."

AT THE DANCE BAR:
"Pocketing a gun, or are you just glad to dance with me?"

AT THE CONTINENTAL BATHS—BETWEEN BETTE MIDLER SETS:
"Is there someone in this dark corner?"

AT THE STORE WINDOW:
"That marble bust of Golda Meir just caught my eye."

AT THE BAR: FRIENDLY BROTHER APPROACH:
"I've seen you and I've always wanted to tell you how much I like your socks."

AT THE BAR: THE FLASHING CASH APPROACH:
"All I have are hundred-dollar bills."

AT THE BAR: PAST-FAMILIARITY PLOY:
"I was certain you were George Broadbelt from P.S. 73."

AT THE MODERN MUSEUM:
"I have an extra ticket for the movie . . ."

OVER THE DEPARTMENT STORE COUNTER:
"How much do you charge . . . for this tie?"

AT THE PIN BALL, PONG, POOL GAME—IN THE BAR:
"Why you just beat me every single time, you're so good and I'm so little . . . let me buy you a drink."

ON THE BEACH, IN THE WATER:
"How long can you hold your breath?"

AT THE FUNERAL:
"Wild horses wouldn't drag a bad word about him out of me, but . . ."

All right, it's time to try your fledgling wings as a sensuous homosexual human being. Go out this night and cruise! But don't fly too high or too far. Your feathers are not quite dry yet. And won't be until you read the next chapter on erotic awareness and technique. Come home early and . . . go on to the next page.

11

HOW TO DRIVE YOUR LOVER TO ECSTASY: PART I

Whirling colored lights, ringing bells, fireworks in the sky —are descriptions of the greatest satisfaction known to the human race: *sexual ecstasy*. You will learn in this chapter how to drive your partner to it, and chauffeur yourself as well!

Am I about to tell you how to do some pretty mad things?

UmmmmUmmmm. Yes, but not in terms of new positions. (Unless you consider anal fist penetration something new; it isn't, but it is gaining ground in popularity—it has a cachet so I *have* included it.) I'm sure you're aware of all the positions; you could probably show me roll-in-the-hay antics that would turn my hair platinum. What we're going to do is consider the regular positions with renewed enthusiasm, and in the light of what you've learned about mana.

This chapter will give your erotic awareness a booster shot and your sexual technique a tune-up. You'll be fabulous.

You know it is an axiom of art that you have to know the rules of form before you can break them. Sex at its best is spontaneous. And it is my belief that gay people are second to none when it comes to between-the-sheets improvisation. It is *informed spontaneity*, however, that cuts the mustard.

You know "erotic" comes from Eros, the Greek God of Love. Erotic means devoted to or tending to arouse sexual love or desire. Lovely phrases. I hope you have a sense of history. When next you jump in bed for sex, remember it's an ancient Greek tradition that you're keeping alive. Yes, you. And in view of that, you want to perform as an eroticist par excellence: passionately, yet gracefully. You're learning to do it in this book. You're going to make both you and your sex mate ecstatically happy. And happiness, no matter what you've heard, is sexual passion, not a warm puppy.

The matter of terminology is touchy. You'd be amazed how much research I've put into deciding what words to use to name the various positions. I hate cutesy-pooh phrases like "The Butterfly Flick" or "The Silken Swirl" or "The Whipped Cream Wriggle." Eccch! But as I've mentioned, "active" and "passive" are too colorless. So, I've decided upon "dominant" and "submissive"—words that cover the subject adequately and have more gut appeal.

About role-playing—I've said I think it's liberating to settle on your more-than-not role. But don't settle on it without having tried all the roles. Consider roles as ex-Governor Rockefeller considers his possible future as President—keep your options open. It would be hell to limit yourself unnecessarily. To go sexually hungry for no reason. Remember what Mame said: "Life is a banquet and all those poor bastards out there are starving." She's right: in your unceasing search for sexual gratification, you must leave no bed unchurned.

And one final observation.

You are now a freed son of the new generation, regardless of your age. In this new generation, sexual barriers are collapsing. You can't use social disapprobation as an excuse anymore for your sexual faint-heartedness. You've got to get in there and f--- (fight, of course). You do if you want to leave life—when it comes time—with a smile on your lips.

Let's begin this chapter with a consideration of the cause of it all—your penis—and then on to the classy duo stuff.

The Penis

The size of your penis, length or width, is a moot point. You have what you have—no amount of esoteric manipulation or arcane exercise procedure is going to change that—you do your best with it to please. There are gays who can't exist without an oversize penis to cuddle up to at night ("Thy rod and thy staff to comfort me"—I wonder which was which). Those gays are simply not for you or you for them if your penis is average, so forget them. If your penis is less large than average, it is incumbent upon you to make up for what you lack in inches by prowess in performance. Compensate! (Always a valid dictum.) If, though, you *are* oversize in the penis department and by chance haven't a host of devoted admirers, you may have to forgo sex with certain willing but incapable individuals; you'll strengthen your capacity for sacrifice, a neglected virtue. I must say that usually your partner can find *something* to do with it.

If penis size is a pressing consideration in your own sexual arrangements, you must case baskets with especial avidity before inviting someone home. Surely, by now, you're able to distinguish the real thing from padding. At bars, stand near the jukebox; that gives you better light. Don't forget that some penises look like nothing in repose, but in action . . . ah! the Washington Monument. Similarly, some penises of noble potential in repose remain potential still, erected.

Kissing

I have rhapsodized previously on the desirable quality of the *first* kiss you share with a lover. And now I want to say every kiss must be so deep, so true, so poignant that when you release each other you are both dizzy. Unless you're dashing out the door to your office; if you kiss like that each time, you'll never make it.

When you kiss, are your lips soft and burning (never hard and dry)? Do you *open those lips just slightly*, receptive to his gently probing tongue? (Moist tendril of delight: you remember from your exercises.) Is your kiss a gesture of your whole being, not just a movement of your head? (It should be a gesture of your whole being.) And when you are in the mouth-to-mouth resuscitation phase of a kiss, does your body meld with his? Again, it should, if you mean business. Neither a crowbar nor an indiscreet interruption ought to be capable of prying you apart. An indiscretion factor can enhance the kiss if it doesn't actually put a stop to it. I've seen kisses which, because they were stolen in a bar or at a party, were mightily passionate.

A kiss should be a fuse for sex. Kissing should start in both your brains a whirring sensation—the machinery of primitive drives soon to be slaked. A serious kiss is a commitment of self down to the ground. The only exception I can think of might be at the beginning of a love affair, when two lovers kiss each time they pass in the apartment; roughly at five-minute intervals (all right, three-minute ones). It's difficult to make a kiss a commitment of self and prelude to sex every single time. It isn't? Right on, baby!

The Princeton Rub

I said I abominated cutesy-pooh names for sexual positions, and I promised you not to use them. The Princeton Rub, however, (hereafter referred to as the PR) is a real name.

You will find the PR useful if your partner is relatively inexperienced but much enamored of you: oddly enough for an attribute you *do* possess but which he idealizes beyond possibility. He looks up to you as a mentor. (You can see that the PR lends itself to and possibly originated in a collegiate situation.) Anyway, unconsciously he wants you passionately, but his inexperience puts him at cross-purposes with himself. He can hardly talk, much less fuck, in your company. His looks? He is a blond, dreamy, perfectly fed and reared specimen of the upper-middle or even wealthy class of people. His clothes are a studied style in carelessness. His accoutrements are in superb taste; you know- —everything that comes to his hand is the best or most efficient there is. He is an extremely attractive and truly elegant boy. You know exactly what his mother is like because he imitates her charming, nostalgic gestures with precision. He is the very prototype of a princely Princetonian.

Your PR sex together will have a lengthy immediate prelude. It will be (to jump the gun), a result of a long bull session with him about LIFE. The session may last ten, twelve hours, which you can hardly spare, but which you feel you want to invest in the boy because LIFE is such a problem for him, and you've got an erection just imagining what it's going to be like holding him. You can ease the time of the prelude with good advice and relatively small amounts of weed and liquor. Not too much of either because, in his nervous condition, he'll pass out on you at the drop of a pie plate.

It is now the eleventh consecutive hour of your conversation, the room is littered with debris from your makeshift dinner, books and papers you both have referred to, and his shoes, which are off. For the last two hours the topic has been the life of F. Scott Fitzgerald. You both have decided that, indeed, he was the spring God who died young, and who took wit and romance with him. It is two a.m. and you're exhausted but determined and you rejoice to see that he is weakening. He slurs his words and his fawn eyes are not focusing properly. By this time you are sitting side by side on the couch and your legs have been in contact for the last twenty minutes. The pressure from his side is so great that your thigh muscle is growing tired just resisting. Your arm over the back of the couch behind him is tingling with loss of circulation but, as I said, you're determined. Suddenly (not a word having passed between you for five minutes) he leans close to you and mumbles he's gotta go. With all the will power you possess, you must indicate that you have heard and that you are neither dismissing him nor bidding him to stay. You know that in his unconscious undergraduate mind the wheels are working; he is close to his moment of truth. He leans closer and closer to you, your arm slides down around him from behind, and you kiss, long and well.

As he withdraws, you notice his eyes have come alive and have taken on an inward look: he is no dummy, nor is he a coward. He straightens up and says something to the effect: well, we've gone this far, we might as well go all the way. All the way for him consists in landing squarely on top of you (both fully dressed), getting you on your back and ravishing your face with wet kisses that contain the pent-up ardour of a boy of eighteen who's been deprived of sex most his life.

The Princeton Rub begins. He's kissing you sloppily, his arms and legs are wrapped around you (ruining your outfit, which you'd hoped to wear tomorrow). Your obligation here is to make the moment as esthetically beautiful for the boy as you can. Kissing and hugging preponderate—real sex is out: he'd never understand. You lie together each by each, rubbing erection against erection through sport jackets, pants, shirt tails, underwear tails and jockey shorts. He considers it the ultimate in illicit copulation. His inward look, which you observed earlier, will change in the next few months to a faraway look as he wanders meditatively about the campus. Shades of F. Scott! But back to our scene:

When he's come and you've come, not twenty minutes after you began, prepare for a sour expression on those perfect features—ugh, the sticky stuff—as he pulls himself together. You see him to the door: he is once again manly and elegant and he despises you. You may expect a telephone call from him in three days. After all, for him, you have mana.

Mutual Masturbation

Less elementary than the Princeton rub but still over-simple, mutual masturbation can be refreshing: a back-to-basics ploy.

You undress together, kissing and caressing enroute. Naked, you fondle his genitals as he fondles yours. This can be accomplished standing in front of a mirror (which gives you the titillating effect of a third-party voyeur) or lying down face to face while hands work busily below. Or it can be done in the position I prefer. Both of you sit on the bed, cross-legged, facing and close. Each of you can see what's going on, and you can kiss. It may sound awkward, but it's quite comfortable. Ernest Hemingway, I suppose, would have called it mano a mano (hand to hand)—he so loved things Spanish!

Expertly fondle: your hands move slowly down his thighs until they touch the target, and starting from the bottom, caress his scrotum (gently, gently), then through the pubic hair like rabbits through the grass, and on to the bullseye (his penis, of course). A firm, light pressure to begin with and many reverse courses back to the scrotum, and manipulation from the base with a side-to-side movement of the penis, as if it were the boom of a sailing boat, free in the wind. This can last a long while, and should, indeed. You ought to be able to bring him nearly to climax several times (and he's doing the same for you, naturally). Meanwhile, your free hand is running over as much of his body as you can reach (and his free hand, etc.). Your heads must seem to be permanently joined at the lips, exchanging mana.

This is a moment for lubricant. I haven't gone deeply into lubricants because I am so biased in favor of Vaseline. And I still believe, despite its potential for staining sheets, that it facilitates the best slurpy fuck. Reminds me of what J.P. Morgan, I think it was, told the man who asked how much it cost to keep Morgan's yacht. J.P. answered that if you have to ask how much it cost to maintain, you shouldn't own such a yacht in the first place. My answer to anyone who complains about Vaseline stains on sheets, is that they shouldn't be having sex in the first place! There are other lubricants, notably K.Y. But it is absorbed by the skin so fast, that you're left with dry flesh and muscle against a dry hand or dry anus—as abrasive as a fingernail against a blackboard. I know a devotee of Bain de Soliel, and it smells nice, but at two dollars a tube . . . and when you're in the midst of a sexual congress you're hardly in the mood to give the tube a delicate squeeze or start at the bottom of the tube the way you're supposed to. I have noticed that the dirty-book stores are carrying sexual curios and accessories these days—similar to Brentano's stocking jewelry and sculpture—and that they have for sale some wicked-looking jams and jellies that purport to be lubricants. I've never tried any.

Back to our mano-a-mano lovers. The application of the lubricant is a small ceremony in itself. Apply it gently and proportionately even more gently (until you're almost patting it on) as his penis (and yours) stiffens for the final event. I've always found it interesting to watch how an engorged penis turns almost blue-black with excitement. But, like looking at the splendor of a sunset, one hardly has time to appreciate the phenomenon before it has passed.

Throbbing—and possibly dripping—penises in hand, now is the time for increasing your hand pressure around his (and his, yours) and accelerating the beat. The mood between you has the drama of men watching gauges in the control room before rocket blast-off. The pace quickens, lips and arms fasten tightly and you're beating him off as he madly jerks you; come flies—don't stop—until his last dribble wends its tiny way down the back of your hand. Now you can fall over exhausted, and surreptitiously reach down for the towel—if you really are concerned about those sheets.

A Serendipitor's Journey

Serendipity means the gift of finding valuable or agreeable things not deliberately sought. It is the general name under which I'm going to lump sexual foreplay. In describing the major sexual positions (next chapter) I shall take it for granted that you will engage in serendipity without having to be reminded each time. Your tongue becomes your walking stick.

It's hard to imagine that there's any place on the human body not explored for erogenous possibility. But on the serendipitor's journey that you're about to take, let's say that there *are* a few places to be found along less well-traveled paths or, off the beaten saliva trails.

1. His toes. Each more delicious than the last, especially the little toe. Separate and suck—like eating artichokes. Don't forget to lick between the toes. You've said you love the ground he walks on—here's your chance to prove it! Warning: Hold On To That Foot. As he writhes in pleasure, he'll kick, and you don't want to be the first one ever to take a whole foot in your mouth.

2. His knee-caps! First tongue a kneecap until it's slippery. With your fingers extended but held together, press them against his kneecap, slowly splaying them as you do: the sensation is a delicate one, but exquisite: you shall have shown yourself capable of a connoisseur's gesture. And while you're serendipiting in that area, don't forget behind his kneecap, in back (of his leg). Your whole face should follow your tongue in there, with kisses.

3. His fingers. You want his fingers always limber, and you can help with that as well as excite him. Suck each one thoroughly, as you did his toes, and in-between. Then give a gentle tug on each finger, as if it were a cow's teat. Sometimes you can hear the joint crack, sometimes not. Milking his fingers has a soothing effect on him; it's as if his tension were being drained off from his fingertips. Remember to take all his fingers in your mouth at once, prelude to his penis, and for heaven's sake, before you leave the vicinity, lick the palms of his hands

teasingly: those palms are real tickle spots on some people, so don't be surprised if he giggles. You do not play generally for giggles during sex, but do—just this once.

4. His armpits. A point of interest that you must dive into head first to fully enjoy. His armpits are wonderful, because they're his, of course, and you care for him. To carry along the serendipity analogy, think of his armpits as hanging gardens. Their dampness, their fragrance of natural things—his armpits are like a secluded bower of green-growth. No one will bother you here; relax and enjoy.

5. The Nose. Unless your sex partner is Cyrano de Bergerac (in which case the nose requires even greater attention), the nose offers the serendipitor a challenge. Your object with the nose is to enslave it without alienating it; cover it with your lips so that he has an erotic, submerged sensation, but don't remain its captor so long that he feels he's about to drown. It's a thin line, but it can be done. If this is your first bed bout with him, perhaps it would be best to skip it: you don't want him dead in the water.

6. The Back of His Neck. A sheer voyage of discovery. If he's trendy, the back of his neck hasn't been seen for a half a dozen years. It's yours to find and to claim! He must cooperate by lying on his stomach. Lovingly, brush the forest of hair aside, and behold! you are master of all you survey! And it's as clean and fresh as a Caribbean beach. Aren't you glad you came! Lick and kiss all you want, and go right around to the backs of his ears. You've staked the territory, explore it: it's yours!

7. Analingus. I shall end this section with the most marvelous serendipitor's journey of all. I cannot but feel that it is the rough sexual equivalent of a trip to America's Grand Canyon.

It's certainly true that most of the great wonders of the world have become such clichés that the tasteful traveler is repelled. One would not willingly go out of one's way to see the Grand Canyon, or Niagara Falls or New York's Botanical Gardens. Oh, you might if you had a little nephew or niece in tow, or your out-of-town cousin of seventy who'd never before left her home town in Lima, Ohio, and the wonder was close by.

Having said that, I shall now describe to you a *super-tourist*. *He* works on the theory inherent in the old story about a visitor who goes to view the Mona Lisa in the Louvre. It is *not* the painting that is being judged; it is *his* capacity for appreciation of the masterpiece that is on trial.

Analingus, in short, is a well-traveled route. What you get out of your visit depends upon your unspoiled capacity for appreciation.

You must go prepared for a longish stay, and during your stay, frequent withdrawals and replungings to the depths from the buttocks' perimeter. Unfortunately, many serendipidists are overwhelmed by the buttocks' perimeter and they never do travel to the bottom. Don't you be one of those who's lured from the main attraction.

Set, go, descend! Your trusty tongue walking-stick precedes you, finding a tongue-hold here and a tongue-hold there, here a hold, there a hold—everywhere! Thrilling! The pressure drop alone makes you giddy. If that happens, rest and view the smoothe alabaster canyon walls stretching above you as far as the eye can see! Some people tout *cunnilingus* as a better attraction; a toss-up, a matter of taste. All right, you've tarried long enough; recommence your pilgrimage before you lose momentum. Fairly soon, depending on whether you took the upper or lower entry trail, you should be in sight of your reward for the arduous descent—the magic forest and the quivering, fabled, hole-of-the-deep! At its nearness, many's the tourist to this realm who's lost control, succumbed to a fit of madness, dived in willy-nilly! Dilettantes! Having gone so far, they might try for a bridled enthusiasm, a measured approach. Now you are at the rim of the fabulous hole. Inch by inch, your tongue-stick as your Virgil, you circumnavigate the rim many times to get the full enjoyment. Then, only then, should you act with all the passion that is in you and. throw yourself down into the hole, which opens slightly to receive you. Oh mana as you go! Oh fabulous rapture!! Excelsior!!! Once visited, this valley of delights may become for you a Shangri-La. It may take all your will power to keep you from returning and wanting to spend your life there. Many indeed are the serendipidists who have not returned. Perhaps they have found there all they ever need. Judge them? Not I!

Note: If you've never been on the receiving end of analingual activity, you never have had sex. Get with it, or join your cousin in Lima.

12

HOW TO DRIVE YOUR LOVER TO ECSTASY: PART II

While you've been on your delectable serendipitor's journey, where do you think your partner's been? Out of this world—*where you put him!* You think you've been tripping—he's been on a trip and a half. Ecstatic!

If we could implant one of Mr. Nixon's famous telephonic bugs in your partner's brain, the monologue would go something like this: "Oh, oh, I'm close, no, no, not yet, more, more, a little to the left, I can't stand it, I'll come, no, it's too good, I'll die, more, further down, where's he going, Jesus, I didn't know I could feel anything there! more, More, MORE!"

After years of nightly research in the field, I have concluded that there are five basic positions for gay sex. You'll drive your lover to ecstasy *by sucking him off, by having him suck you off, by having him fuck you, and by your fucking him.* (We're getting to know one another; I feel I can be direct.) But I said five positions. The fifth one, and the most venerable, is, of course, *"69"*. Since it *is* such a venerable position—and the subject of dreary ridicule from rednecks, gay and otherwise—let's begin with it.

"69"

By decision or accident, you and your lover end up lying foot to head, head to foot. (Aren't you glad I told you about kissing-sweet feet!) From that stance, you both ease down until you are vis-a-vis his penis and he, yours. Your tongue surges like a brush fire through his pubic region; his tongue surges similarly. You let his penis nuzzle your face, meander through your hair; he does likewise. You lick his balls (remember your exercise with that soggy peach) as he licks yours—you'll have a very good time. Hold tight to his thighs, he'll buck and pitch with pleasure-torment, exactly as you are doing: neither you nor he want to come uncoupled. Ablaze with passion, gurgling sensual gurgles, you explode in each other's mouths.

Here I must carp. I can think of few times in my life when I enjoyed old "69." I find myself either too far up or too far down from where my mouth ought to be for easy access by his penis. I have almost dislocated a shoulder trying to balance my body weight either on top of him or to one side. I have risked broken ribs by attempting to support my partner's weight. And I cannot concentrate on the sucking at hand while my partner is busy and efficient at his task below. I share redneck sentiment about "69." I'm told—and I believe—that the position is mutuality incarnate: mana made easy. Luck to you.

You as Submissive Partner: Oral

Unlike your serendipitor's journey (properly circumlocutious), the approach here for best triggering pinwheels of fire in your partner's brain is long and low but straight-arrow. You commence descent below his nose, drop your tongue in the cleft of his chin (or below his lower lip if he be cleftless), trail swiftly down his neck, evenly between his nipples, keeping up the pace and leaving no doubt in his mind that you are on course for orgasm. Touch down below his belly button and sweep right into the pubic brush. Taxi along, under and around—then bounce or pounce on the phallic runway. By this time he should be moaning low, the pinwheels turning for him faster and faster. By no means accede—and here we drop the flight analogy—to a sudden, sodden gobbling of territory so carefully staked out. You might do a sensual pirouette here: flick your tongue above and about his corona like a moth around a flame. His moans should now have become sighs, quite loud, shading off into breathy grunts. Whether you can see it or not, you know his penis is changing color from hard-red to gun metal blue-black and certainly you can feel it stiffen. And you're aware by the taste that one little pearl of come has harbingered its way into your mouth. At that, begin the beguine: he's about ready. Teeth sheathed by firm lips, slide up and down the tubular treasure. He may want to engage in light ramming—steady your grip with one hand at the base of his penis. With the other, caress his scrotum and let your hand wander below to his anus where you may find a finger-hold that is warm and welcoming. He murmurs he's coming: the parade is in sight! Don't lose your head here, *or his*. Keep your lips air-tight on his penis, for suction and to avoid seed-spilling, a heinous sin according to the great good book. If, in the mounting lustful craze, the head of his penis should escape your lips, there ought to be a popping sound attesting to your lips' seal-test prowess. As he tells you in no uncertain terms that he's about to deliver mana, you may want to aid his sperm-release by hand-strokes; your job is utter fidelity to stroke and rhythm. And now the hot load is yours spurt after spurt after spurt! He is, thanks to you, at one with creation! Your mouth is filled to overflowing but—don't make a move! Or only the slightest move, to swallow. Retain the wonder-stick until every come-drop has been extracted. Release him when you sense he is inert above you, and his penis has melted in your mouth.

You as Dominant Partner: Oral

You, as suckee, are in a position to give your partner a different sort of treat. You're going to sock it to him, and even while he's gagging and choking he'll be begging for more. As sucker (that's him), your partner wants nothing less than to eat the whole thing—your penis, your come, and your totally engaged body and mind. Commence by strongly taking the lead: punish him if he misses a beat by briefly depriving him of your penis. Sexpertise is a double thread. One aspect of pleasing your partner is to thoroughly please yourself. After the preliminaries, use his mouth as an orifice of your delight and passionate ferocity. Grab him by the head or by the ears, and pace his pigeon-necked perambulations. As suckee, this is your party, and the more you make it so, the better he likes it. Although he is the submissive partner here, let's say that between the two of you, *he*, again, has mana. (Remember I said that either the dominant or submissive partner could have mana. He has it and you want to fuck it out of him.) Using the implanted bug again, but in *your brain*, the monologue might go like this: "Damned little self-possessed pretty queen, who the hell do you think you are, suck my dick, baby, when I let you or tell you to, now baby, get on it and take it deep, deep so that you choke, bitch." You might augment the action with a little furrily muttered speech. He'd love a recording of it, if you're half the sensuous homosexual I think you are, (remember your margin of hostility). For him, it's a kind of mud-bath effect. But you're close; command him to take your penis deep; ram it home and give him the elixir of life he thirsts for; he'll languish back on the bed satiated and serene (note that look of gratification on his face). Oh, I forgot—before he falls back, for heaven's sake let go his ears! And afterward, kiss him.

You as Submissive Partner: Anal

There you are in a classic prone position: leaning over the arm of your new sofa, buttocks ready. You have mana this time and your sex mate is a brawny older man—in fact, a member of the team of furniture movers from Bloomingdales who delivered the sofa that morning. He accepted the invitation you slipped him on paper along with the twenty. He arrived at seven and you wined and dined him at home and listened endlessly to his wife-and-kids maneuver until you thought you'd expire from boredom and that you'd made a mistake. But no, he was milking you for sympathy (mana) about the whole of his misdirected life. Suddenly you're both stripped and, without the love-making you'd hoped for, he's right into the action. He's pure muscle and he has the thrust of an Atlas missile. You'll please him most by rotating your buttocks (Exercise No. 6)—up and down, left to right and in a circle as he plunges his weapon deep. Beg him for verbal abuse; it'll do him good and you might learn a thing or two for when you're dominant again. He is untiring; you feel as if it's you he's been saving up for in terms of sexual energy. Relax, let him penetrate you profoundly; then close that sphincter muscle of yours tight and feel his fabulous shaft like the drill-head of an oil-derrick. Your anus is obviously what *he's* been searching for all these years, and he's not going to give it up without leaving his mark, which may mean a little of your blood on the towel that he thoughtfully went and got to put under you to save the new sofa. Unable to hold back any longer, you come. Then that heaving mountain of man (splitting you in two) comes . . . and comes . . . and comes. Making twice in one day he's delivered you a load. He leaves shortly, but you know you'll see him again. First, he said you were the best he ever had (he'll come back); second, you haven't told him, but you're returning that sofa!

You as Dominant Partner: Anal

Now we'll put *you* on the firing end and also equip you with mana. If, by the assignment of so much facility, you feel an upsurge of God-likeness, enjoy! (Controlled inflation is acceptable.) Captivated from the bar or from the party by your sensual aura, he is naked and in bed. (No gloating.) Your job is to make him happy. If he's a new friend (one hour), it's going to require a mite of probing to find out how. Artful, if not crafty, improvisation is the key. The lock is the correct positioning of his buttocks for anus entry that resembles a straight super-highway rather than a tortuous country road. The obvious position is the gay counterpart of the straight world's so called-missionary position—one atop the other: your partner face down beneath you, ready for penetration. Boring and dated. Try him for real on his back, knees raised slightly, legs spread apart, hips thrust forward. Kneel between his hungry thighs, lubricate both his anus and your penis, and enter according to his natural trajectory. Like most human copulating positions, it is not dignified. Especially if in this position your partner's legs fold over your shoulders in clutch action or his feet brace against your shoulders for spring action. My preference as the dominant partner is to have mon ami sitting on my penis as I lie back and revel. Usually possible and comfortable for the submissive partner, this position allows maximum activity for both. Beaucoup kissing—and I can reach and manipulate him. Also, since he's on top and I'm pinned, so to speak, he can promote the situation, which I don't mind a bit. Back to you—you've got mana on this go-around and, as you begin penetration, you must rejoice in your strength (wallow in it, consciously). You've got what he wants, so, baby, give it to him. Once you've entered your tempo is faster and faster, emerging fully a few times only to re-establish for him the wonder of your initial thrust. If your penis slips its groove unduly, you can be sure you haven't got a virgin. In and out, round and about—that's the spirit: bounce his butterball buns! Attuned as you are to each other, he mentally telegraphs the message that he's getting close. You make your thrusts more urgent, you go deeper into his rectum—as you reach for the poppers: one for each. He hitches his legs over your shoulders and around your neck for clutch action and the mutual response is wild! Dual climax is assured with your hand pumping his penis so rapidly you're concerned you'll skin it! If ever sexual partners resembled horse and rider at a bronco-busting exhibition, it's right this minute! Wham! Socko! Pow!

Turn out the lights and go to sleep.

Fist Penetration

Fist-fucking is to gay life what anal penetration is to heterosexuality (in America, at least): a relatively unexplored area of sexual endeavor; no longer shocking, and gaining acceptance and respectability in the suburbs as well as the city. I admit that I have *not* been fist-fucked. Some special friends, (experts at "different strokes," proselytizers all) tell me that I don't know what I'm missing. Maybe. I feel the same way about it as I do about a summer visit to Anchorage, Alaska; I'd rather sweat it out in New York and take a bus on Saturday to areas 1 and 2 at Riis Park. But I *have been* the assiduous donor of my fist, wrist, forearm and, yes, my elbow to a devotee of the practice, so I feel qualified to speak from that limited point of view. I am glad to report that there is an inimitable, ribald cachet to the experience. On the one hand, as it were, it's a lesson in anatomy first hand (hands keep cropping up here), and on the other, or *with* the other, you can masturbate your partner—doubling his pleasure, doubling his fun. Language during F-F is an enormous assist, relieving his tension and providing you with a sort of control-tower guide for the passage of your blind—and groping—progress toward the interior. You must consider his primal scream as the signal that you've gone far enough. Dangerous, of course—tearing inner tissue because you forgot to do your nails or remove your wrist-watch; clumping unhandily against his various organs as you go. The chief demurer I would put on this particular different stroke is that it is somewhat tedious to watch—one is, perforce, a voyeur. But it cannot be dismissed out of hand (hands again) for that reason. *He* is pleasured—*that* must be the important criterion of any bit of sexual derring-do, hands down. Or up. Or in. Where-ever.

Simultaneous Anal Penetration

In the interest of completeness I suppose I must mention this execrable practice. A seemingly impossible feat, it is accomplished by two partners on all fours, facing away from each other, cheek to cheek, literally! One end of a flexible plastic hose, two feet or so long, contoured and colored to look like a two-headed penis, is inserted by each of the partners into his own anus. By rocking back and forth in their all-fours position, each is rewarded with the sensation of being fucked by the other. I've assayed this position and must report to you, it isn't convincing. Debasing mechanization! I could throw up. And to think, plastic is almost indestructible—whatever will archeologists of the future think of us when they find one of those gimcracks among the artifacts!

Those Different Folks; Their Different Strokes: *S* and *M*

We must admit there's a little *S* and *M* in all of us. Can you honestly say that a pair of black leather jeans hasn't caught your eye? Or a well-turned boot? Or a singularly studded epaulet? Of course you can't. (I don't care for the little black leather hats on the older gentlemen of this persuasion, but there's always the bad with the good.) And who of us can cast the first stone when it

comes to fantasies: Have you never drawn mental pictures show-
ing a trick tied to the rack? Or being whipped with a six-prong?
Or at least being forced to his knees, with hands tied behind
—begging for mercy? For shame if you haven't: you didn't read
the right comic books as a child. The right ones espoused every
conceivable torture and one was qualified after reading them for a
job as a Spanish Inquisitor. Hurrah if you did read them, and
admit to it; your mental library under *S* and *M* has contributed
richly to your nightmares and vindictive day-dreams! The only
difference, then, between ourselves and our *S* and *M* friends, is
that they act out with courage and histrionic ability what most of
us horde mentally as masturbatory visual aid material.

Again, as with adherents of cruising butches, the adherents of
S and *M* (openly) are a fairly small group. *S* and *M* people are
dedicated. Even a caricatured re-enactment of the ancient
Judaeo-Christian myth of guilt and expiation requires *time, cash
and savvy*. I feel I must cover the subject—in however cursory a
fashion—because *you may want to dabble–or have a lover, or a
trick, who can be driven to ecstasy only by S and M procedures*.
For you to have to say "What!?" when he attempts to cleanse
you with a golden shower or engage you in more strenuous disci-
plinary activity is unthinkable to your presently evolving status as
a sensuous homosexual.

I must prepare you at the outset for the expense. To "do" the *S*
and *M* scene requires costly gear. With no thought of price for
torture implements, the costumes alone of leather and metal can
run you a mint. And the boots!—a fortune. Alas, it is *all required*
equipment, like the things your parents had to include in your
pack when you went off as a child to formal summer camp. At
most *S* and *M* bars, the leather costume is as de rigeur as black tie
in Palm Beach—my dear, you will be turned away at the door if
you don't comply and you will hooted out if you to attempt to
force an entrance wearing a fluffy sweater! No way! Leather,
then, is your first investment. But don't—repeat, don't—begin

payments on a six thousand dollar motorcycle (or bike, as *S* and *M'ers* say) until you find out what the scene is and whether or not you're really going to dig it.

A friend of mine who used to be my apartment rental agent (there's a transition for you: rental agent to *S* and *M* bar manager) reassures everyone that once you're *inside* his bar things will be easier. When queried as to what his chain-festooned customers talk about, he answered, "The same subjects gay people always talk about—curtains, hair spray and handbags." Chances are, even if you're not conversant with *S* and *M* parlance, you'll get along with your basic English. When in doubt, ask. Yes, *for God's sake* ask for a plainly worded statement of whatever it is your newfound *S* and *M* partner wants you to do to him, or what *he* wants to do to *you*! It could be a messy surprise!

All right, you've found a partner and you've gone home with him. The games begin. No, no—do *not* disrobe! And do *not* express surprise at his place, especially that inner sanctum room he has ushered you into. Pretend that you think every middle-class American home has a 14th-century dungeon cell replete with wall handcuffs, a rack (of course), and various other indispensible accoutrements for inflicting pain and humiliation. (Actually, some cocktail parties you've been to hosted by perfectly respectable people have been far more destructive to your identity than anything that will happen here.) Be nonchalant.

S and *M* is complex, but essentially you will perform as either *master* or *slave*. Prepare yourself by summoning up what you can of the talent for the theater that you thought you possessed when the audience at your high school play clapped so appreciatively as you took your bow. You'll need every bit of it.

You, As Slave.

Begging for mercy, groveling, howling with mingled terror and rapture are the simple ploys on your part that will warm your partner's heart. The evidence of rope burns on your wrists, cigarette burns on your chest, heat blisters on the soles of your feet are the proud insignia of your rank here. The more subservient and verbally self-diminishing you can be at this, the better your dear partner can wrest from the experience his sweet fulfillment. *Do not*, under any condition, let him know or feel that he has *really* hurt you—it would turn him off instantly if he is a sadist of taste and acumen. If he isn't . . . ah well, let's hope he is. At his moment of climax, however peculiarly achieved, you are expected to transmit to him your surrender to his utter mastery. If you need mental pictures of horror, picture how your high-school audience with all the family in the front row would respond to this skit! Bravo! Bravo! And encore!

You, As Master.

Mutuality in sex assumes many guises. As *S* and *M* sex clearly reveals, kicks aren't always a 50/50 deal. As master in these circumstances, you will not disrobe entirely; some deliciously fetichistic article of your apparel remains in place—your bullet belt or your studded black jacket, or perhaps your leather jockstrap, or all of those plus a chic black hood with eye-slits that slant cruelly, such as any fashionable executioner would wear. And two other requirements: hope that your flaying arm hasn't a hitch in the back swing (golf problem) and, of eminent importance, be sure you have not relieved your bladder for three hours previous to this engagement—he is sure to want a urinary specimen. He will instruct you where and when to bestow it. He may also want a defecatory specimen, but if you can't, you can't—masochists of taste understand. Now lay into him hard, and demand all the delectable crawling, whining and cringing from him that you can extract by violence. Be the beast you were in masturbatory adolescent day-dreams to the sexy boy who lived next door. Flailing him with a bicycle chain, demand that the bastard acknowledge you machismo ruler of the world! He'll come and you'll come on him and you've pleased him beyond measure—he may even hang from the wall cuffs around his wrists for a few minutes to get the full benefit—and that's all, basically, there is to it. Oh, certainly, with star actors and elaborate props—guillotines, life-sized wooden crosses, iron maidens and the like—the procedure can have many nuances and refinements, and can be prolonged "for days" (as the kids say). But unless you want to make a career or it (another sort of Shangi-La existence for some), you've now been advised enough to pick your pilgrim's-way wisely among those different folks with different strokes . . . whom we now reluctantly leave (with garlands around our necks) as our cruise ship sets course into the setting sun. Aloha!

*   *   *

With the conclusion of this chapter—here—I award you the degree of *Sensuous Homosexual Human Being!*, or Bachelor of Sex. You have satisfactorily completed the program of study that has led to that honor. *First*, you have learned how to make your partner feel loved as he's never felt loved before—by proving to him that he is uniquely and supremely sexually attractive. You will always possess that genius, to dispense to worthy partners as you will. *Second*, your aura is burnished to glowing, your erotic sensibility is honed to microscopic sharpness, your sexual technique has been reclaimed and perfected. Yours is the ready potential for total sexual fulfillment with anyone, anytime, anywhere that you may care to designate. You have been a cum laude student! Congratulations!

If you must stop reading, I'll understand. I would be less than frank, however, if I did not inform you that there is a further degree (Master of Sex) attainable and much more to learn about sensuous homosexuality and about yourself as a sensuous homosexual human being. I certainly would encourage you to continue, to try for your Master's, to expose yourself to many thrills and delights not yet encompassed, if you would become a *super-sensuous homosexual*. You say that you *are* ready and willing? Excellent!! Let us proceed.

13

LANGUAGE IN GAY ACTION IN BED

Breathes there a gay with soul so dead/Who never to his partner has said: "Fuck me!".

Fuck, suck, bitch, cocksucker, eat it, rim baby are not bad words during the sex act. How *could* they be? These words are the language of sex. Highly desirable in context. If you use them, and encourage your partner to use them, you're adding to sex a necessary spicy ingredient.

Dirty words in bed can give *direction*.

Perhaps something like this has happened to you:

You've got him home, he fits your idea of a "man." You're in bed together and the first few minutes are wild. There's a brief pause, you're hoping he'll take the lead—and, he does (but not the kind of lead you had in mind). He begins tonguing you—from the top, and as he gets to your penis you're thinking you wanted to do that to him. Suddenly you lose your erection. With effort, he manages to get it up again—you manage it by picturing someone else. You come, and then it's his turn and, dumbstruck with disinterest, you go through with it mechanically. He comes, you play content, both have a cigarette, exchange peripheral personal information. When he asks if you'd like him to stay, you answer in a voice filled with distress that you'd love it, but that with someone in bed next to you you just can't sleep, and tomorrow's an early day. You are relieved when he puts on his clothes, writes his name and number in a matchbook cover, kisses you and departs. You rearrange the bed, set the clock (you don't have to rise—that early) and, in a mood of dissatisfaction, you lie back and decide to chalk it up.

What went wrong?

You didn't follow through, good friend, with the necessary language. You practically told him in the bar that you liked to get fucked and when it came time in bed you one-upsmanned him with *silence* and played yourself right out of the game. If to be dominated was what you wanted—and that's why you picked him—you should have whispered in his ear, "Fuck me, baby, with that hot cock''—and then been all over his body. *It is mostly up to the submissive partner to call the shots with erotic language.* The dominant partner's ego is fragile; if there's any doubt, you've got to help him. If you refuse to help, you ain't gonna get laid like you like.

He was aware you wanted him to play the dominant role but also aware that if he zapped you without some indication from you permitting it, you'd have bucked rather than fucked. And you would've. What he is in bed—the first few times, anyway—is what you design him to be. If you shilly-shally, or test him or simply let it ride, the bed story will be as described.

Erotic language is the answer.

If you're submissive, beg him to ram it into you. If you're dominant, tell the pretty bitch what you're going to do to "her." If you're smart, no matter which role you play, you'll make use of language to heighten and shape the sexual experience.

Take it seriously out of bed? Never. Take to heart the names he called you or his tone, feel huffy about it? Absurd. Equally absurd the dominant partner's inclination to really believe he's got the most wonderful cock in the world because he's been told that so many times in bed.

Rough language in bed serves to create that useful *margin of hostility* I mentioned. It provides the space needed between you to express yourselves. Mind-fucking in bed is of equal importance with body fucking. (If you are mind*less* in bed, so will your whole experience be.) The word "laid" does not mean stretched out in the sense of lie down; it means to calm or allay (nerves). If you want your gay nerves thoroughly calmed, you've got to talk your bed partner into sufficient shape to attend to it. With the language of sex, you create the sacred monster in bed that you want to be fucked by, or want to fuck.

Naturally, you've got to feel out a new partner on the subject, as you have felt him out in so much else. If you tell him you don't mind a raw Anglo-Saxon epithet growled in your direction, chances are he'll say he likes it too. Some partners require whole novels of monologue growled in their direction. And sometimes you get a partner who is propriety personified during dinner, but who, when you get him in bed, is more foul-mouthed than a constipated truck driver (long haul).

Remember, dirty words are sexy at the right time in the right place. And they can make of sex experience exactly what *you* want it to be. Good night, Dr. Frankenstein!

P. S. Curiously, in bed after good sex is a time when partners are capable of long perspectives on experience. If you really do feel a fondness for the friend you've just acquired, *in bed after sex is the time to tell him so* and make a date—not when he's got his clothes on and is just leaving; your effort then looks like an afterthought.

P. P. S. In bed after sex is also the time and place to approach and resolve your lover's recent lapse with that little blond hairdresser. And if you both can have a giggle over it (as much as it pained you last week), all the better. There's *no* rule that says that when you get in bed you have to discard your sense of humor along with your yellow nylon bikini briefs. And lastly, bed after sex is a time to reaffirm all the caring and love you feel for your partner, to say all the good and serious things in your heart.

14

HOW TO KEEP THE LOVER YOU ALREADY HAVE

Let's have a Q. and A. session.

Q. Can a gay love affair last?

A. Of course. Few human relationships are as beleaguered by devils within and without as gay love affairs—granted. But with awareness of the problems and some *conscious application of will on your part* toward solution of those problems, a gay love affair *can endure* and be the most constructive and remarkable experience of your life. In this chapter, we'll explore both the problems and the solutions. *I do caution you: it isn't easy.*

Q. Am I a fool and old-fashioned to hold out hope that my one lover will always "stay close"?

A. You are neither. For most of us, no matter how *with it* we are, down deep our emotional life is a search for that *one person* we can, in the best sense, call our own. Pansexuality is the perogative of youth, rightfully so. The young must and should experiment sexually with girls, boys—all positions and every role. When their own pattern of more-than-not sexual responses begins to emerge (at about thirty), it will have a broad and true base in experience, not subject to undue upsets. And *it will some-how include the need for a particular friend.* Gay life in our time may stud itself with sparkling innovations, but the desire for closeness over a long period with *one person* is rooted in the foundation layers of the human psyche.

Q. If it lasts, will my love affair still be fun?

A. If you take care in the ways I'm about to relate, the tenor of your affair can remain light and laughing always—not exactly the same as at the beginning, but better, fuller, *in dimensions you have yet to discover.* I've always been struck with the fact that only straight people who are super-rich can—with elaborate diversion—approximate that easy fun and intimate sharing so natural to gay people in love and in modest circumstances.

Q. All right. What are the how-to's of making secure the love relation I have?

A. Start by defining for yourself what you mean by "love." If it means your possessing someone as you would possess a chair, you must rethink your concept. If it means living your life vicari-ously through the life of your lover, again, you must rethink. If it means using your lover as a whipping post for your daily frustra-tions, rethink. If it means someone you're dependent on finan-cially, rethink. If, on the other hand, *it means someone for whom you feel a tender passion*, for whose welfare in every area of life *you feel utmost solicitude*, you are definitely on the right track. If that tender passion, part of which is always erotic, grows and grows, along with your solicitude, you are moving along that track full-speed.

Q. I understand what is meant by tender passion, but how must I be solicitous?

A. Secure your relationship by giving your lover *room to breathe.* Room to breathe means allowing for and respecting your lover's dark, quirky moods—when you know he loves you but he wants to go for a walk by himself, or listen to a particular record, or write a letter to someone you aren't acquainted with. (He wasn't born, you must realize, the day he met you.) It means arranging a place (if you are living together) that he can call his own; even if it's a corner of a room: a place where you do not go unless invited, or ever pry into when he's not there. And it means, during these quiet times of his, that you find something apart from him to occupy yourself with, preferably outside. Oh, I know, when he withdraws, those are the very moments when your mind is flooded with visions of what the two of you might be doing together. Resist it, let him be. If you don't, he'll probably give in to whatever it is you want to do—and you may even have a great day together. But his need to withdraw will be more urgent the next time, and he will act on it more certainly as it builds in him.

If, on the other hand, you are the one who needs a quiet time, don't just walk out and leave him hanging. Explain your need briefly and caringly and then take your walk. I am not a believer in the adage, "Never Explain, Never Complain" or "Love Is Never Having To Say You're Sorry." *Explanations, complaints and apologies all have their place in human relationships*—and were invented, not to obstruct them, but to work toward their viability. To mend the hundreds of tiny, inevitable breaks in continuity. *So* explain, complain and apologize when the situation warrants. Anyone who does not avail himself of these splicing words frustrates himself and his partner needlessly. *Homosexual love affairs are notable for their intensity. Any separation*, especially as a result of an argument or misunderstanding, *inflicts pain*. The hurt is deep in proportion to the pleasure taken by the lovers in their proximity.

Q. I understand, about giving him—and myself—room to breathe. Another problem that my lover and I have is coping with an insidious monotony. We've been together two years. What can I do?

A. Monotony develops when you begin to measure your relationship *now* against the way it was at the *beginning* (and you may not be aware of what you are doing). Monotony (and panic) develops when you both try desperately to *punch up the pitch* of your relationship to where it was at the start—ignoring the fact that in every human relationship there are changes—peaks and troughs, shade and brilliance, progression and, yes, regression; it is in the nature of things. If you and he bank on the love that you have, and live along patiently, you will be back riding the crest of the wave again before you know it. If, indeed, there really aren't more basic difficulties.

Q. What do you mean "punch up the pitch of your relationship to where it was at the beginning"—what mistakes, exactly, are we making?

A. Lovers try to re-establish the early pitch of their relationship by doing the same things they've always done together, but more often: seeing the same people, going to the same places; believing (or wanting to) that it will all be as it was before if they can only stop time and follow the old routines exactly enough. And it does work, somewhat, for a while. But not very long, or with any real degree of success. The true solution to monotony is the very opposite: *Flee from those early rituals!*

Here are *twelve suggestions* for you when you notice that clenched-teeth expression come over your lover's face, or when you reach the point in your relationship (usually after dinner) when each asks the other, *"What shall we do tonight?"* If my suggestions work for you, fine; I'd prefer it if they stimulated you to invent your own.

1. Let's start modestly. Agree on an interesting book; buy two copies, read it at the same time, and discuss it. Get two water-color sets, paper; go somewhere picturesque and paint together.

2. Ask him what's bothering him. Chances are it has to do not with you but with an aspect of his work—his boss, a troublesome fellow employee, or maybe *his whole career projection needs overhauling*. Be his sympathetic sounding board. That's how people help each other to cope, to grow and be effective.

3. Try working out together: barbells at home; swimming at one of the numerous private clubs or the Y. Bicycling is always fun and great exercise. Tennis, too, is a good bet, and very in. You adore each other's bodies: make it a kind of prolonged foreplay to the sex you'll have when you return home and shower. Or don't shower!

4. If it's at all possible, get away from where you live even for a short weekend. A change of scene works miracles. And/or plan a journey together. Obtain brochures from travel agencies and plan it in detail. Chances are planning will be as much fun as doing it and when you go, you will forget what you planned anyway and explore. But hell, that's two trips for the price of one.

5. Maybe there's *something about you* that's bothering him. Be willing to ask and to change if necessary, but be receptive enough to discuss it. He could be right.

6. Would you believe—try a few minutes of deliberate *meditation* together. Between two people who love each other, silent meditation can be most eloquent and lead to heartfelt communication.

7. I am a propagandist for a regular cocktail or pot-smoking hour before dinner. It divides the day neatly, and gives you the energy of a second morning. You are then fresh to eat and enjoy your dinner, and later, to eat and enjoy your lover!

8. Instead of watching TV until your minds are numb, see a play or a musical or a live nightclub act—and even if you have to drive fifty miles to do it. People performing on a stage have a certain magic drawing power that TV can't approach. Live entertainers can make you forget your problems and it's curious, but one always remembers a play or a musical or a live act that one has seen—hardly ever TV fare.

9. Do that paint job on the living room that you've been meaning to do for so long. After deciding together on color, you go and get the paint, the brushes, etc., so that your lover doesn't

have to—but paint together. Showered and in bed afterwards, you will find sex to be as it may not have been for weeks, or months—fabulous! Damned clever, paint.

10. In addition to the place you both live, an automobile can be a source of mutual pride, pleasure and endeavor. Share the driving even if you don't think he's as expert at the wheel as you are. Daylong trips out of town can also sooth the nerves of both of you. Take friends on a *picnic*. Outdo yourself with the preparations, find a secluded spot, say near a woodsy area, then with your lover . . .

11. Purchase together that article of clothing he's been in need of. You've learned about fit and taste in this book, so you qualify as an objective observer and informed critic. Keep in mind *his* point-of-view. It may be an extravagence, but the two of you should check on the possibility of owning evening clothes. If you do, it might open another world for your mutual participation.

12. Go together to an art gallery, and buy a modestly priced *original picture* that you both can agree on. You'll be delighted how much that picture will mean to you both when it's properly framed and hung.

Q. We're having trouble in bed. Either he doesn't do what he's supposed to do, or I don't, and we fight and nothing happens. How can I solve that?

A. First, are you certain you love each other?

Q. Yes.

A. Then there's no problem between you that can't be solved. I'd suggest that you give up the idea that either one of you is *supposed* to do anything in bed.

Q. But I thought you said that we should find our roles and play them . . .

A. I said that the pattern of your more-than-not role would emerge from your experience. But you must be flexible. Sometimes it can break the emotional-sexual logjam if you abandon your *more* role for the *than-not* role—and I am not just word-juggling. Loosen up, both of you, and play the opposite role with each other for a bit. It may reveal to you both new capacities for sex. Or it may send you back to your previous roles with resounding sighs of relief! Or let it be a playful mish-mash in bed for a change. *The real thing between you will reassert itself, never fear, because it is real.* There's another kind of trouble in bed that happens when one or the other partner is actually changing his more-than-not role while his lover remains the same. Usually the situation between an older man and a much younger person. Submissive more-than-not in the Ganymede stage of his life-—roughly from 17 to 23 years old—the younger lover begins to want to dominate, while the older man wants him to remain the ''cup-bearer'' still. It is one of the hardest and saddest of realities. There is only one answer: the older man must open the door, stand aside, and hope that his young friend will come back of his own free will when he chooses to. Much easier said than done—I know!

Q. We're having trouble out of bed, too. Either I'm doing something he thinks is wrong, or he's doing something just the opposite to the way I think it should be done. We've actually fist-fought over it. What do you make of that?

A. You've arrived at the ''dark night'' stage of your relationship, the point where it either achieves a new dimension or it breaks up. I said earlier that a gay love affair could last, but that it isn't easy. Most gay affairs break up because the partners don't know how to continue after the initial sexual momentum abates somewhat, and life no longer arranges itself.

First, there's nothing wrong with founding a gay love affair on compatible bed relations (complementary sex roles). For better or worse, most gay affairs start that way. The mistake is to believe that sexual expression between you is going to continue between you exactly as it was during the first week. It can't. It can, however, continue at a high pitch for many years.

Two, your relationship has got to shed its cocoon-like aspect, its old format of habit and ritual that was comfortable and devolved on sex. Concentrating only on the sexual tie between you is death. Both partners end up losing whatever mana each had to offer the other because mana has not been refreshed and reinforced by accomplishments outside the relationship. *With no mutual objective interest to channel culturally induced male assertion* (and two gay people are male to the end—drag queens not excepted, but included, etc.) *you and your lover direct assertiveness toward each other*. You're bound to lock horns. Each tries to prove himself right over the most trivial matters: ego battering ego. And *the truth* of the issue at any particular flash-point is forgotten in the mêlée. What a waste! It happens in gay life time after time! The fighting, the break-up, the grief—and then the awful grind of starting over with someone new. Gay life is saddest when it is condemned to a thousand beginnings. That is not the way it must be, but the way it is for so many.

Three, if, after the arguing and fighting and making-up you still love each other—and get along in bed in spite of all—*the thing to do is think of some project in the world that you both can work at*. That will not only *advance your affair*, but also will be meaningful to you both *spiritually*; at the same time, it will involve you *emotionally* and enhance your *material* lives as well. It has got to happen if you are to continue with him and it has got to embrace all those areas of your existence. *Yes, I am talking about some sort of actual business*. The most successful and enduring gay love affairs that I am familiar with have a mutual business endeavor as their base. A silk-screen business; a perfumery; a dental technician supplier; an antiques shop; a chain of beauty shops; a restaurant—I know a pair of lovers who have two restaurants in their home town; an interior design business; an elegant bathroom-fixture shop; a bicycle repair shop; an art gallery, and more.

Q. But didn't they all have money to put in?

A. I have carefully chosen my examples. Not one of them had a dime of their own before they made their decision to begin a business. After the decision, believing it was right, they worked and saved for a start, most of them, or borrowed money by convincing backers of their very worthwhile and well-planned purpose.

Q. Is that what you mean by my relationship having a new dimension? It sounds like a lot to take on.

A. It is something *great* to take on, and it is a way you and your lover can thrive and prosper—together! It does mean enlarging your lives, surrendering the cozy feeling you got catching the 8:40 bus to your secure job. It calls for relinquishing the infinite attention you lavished on your place or furniture. And it means depending on your partner in a real way in the matter of a hundred things to be decided. A business together can unite the two of you deeply and happily. If you love each other—again, *don't be afraid*; direct the assertiveness of which you are both capable *outward*. Create a dream to offer the world and save your souls thereby!

Q. Won't such an arrangement expose us both to many people and spoil our fragile intimacy?

A. Your so-called fragile intimacy was beautiful, but it has served its purpose and now exists only to strangle you both. *Letting go* can be as life-saving a device as *holding on*. Another, far more dynamic, intimacy will replace it, reaching up and down farther than you can visualize beforehand, and allowing you both a free union that will be rich in mana and sustaining on every level. *As broadly functioning individuals, you will feel a finer magic in your relationship than any you may have lost.*

Q. I like the idea of a business venture but I'm not sure I can depend upon my partner. I can't depend upon him to take care of me in bed the way he used to. Know what? I opened the medicine cabinet and found a jar of cold cream which wasn't mine. And he's supposed to be the man in the family!

A. Your image of him as the dominant partner was cracked by a jar of cold cream?

Q. Shaken. I guess I shook *him* up the other day when I beat him at hand wrestling. He was furious! Not as much *man* as he pretends.

A. You're down to the nitty-gritty. You and your lover are attacking each other's sexual roles. Your major mistake is carrying roles out of bed. Be *human* out of bed, have the *courage to accept* your role *in* bed and be smart enough to stop tearing each other down in *or* out of bed. You and your lover get along sexually; leave well enough alone! Once you've got a thing where you want it, it's best to leave it where it is!

Q. I don't understand.

A. The jar of cold cream said to you that your lover was not a "man," as you define that word. And your beating him at hand wrestling made him mad because you weren't (properly) submissive.

Q. I proved I was stronger than him even if I am submissive in bed.

A. Don't you see, your necessary illusions about each other in bed have become distorted out of bed. The "man" image you put up does not exist except in popular song lyrics ("He beats me too, what can I do/Oh my man I love him so"). It riles me that gays delude themselves with that particular image so often: a "man" for them being half violent Mafia gangster, half kind, muscular Tarzan. You force that delusion on your lover and you lose in the process whatever genuine mana strength he, as dominant partner, might have offered.

Q. What about the image out of bed he forces on me?

A. I haven't finished. The dominant partner is involved in distortion too. He is treating a male, *you, out of bed as if he were a female*. A gay chauvinist, he's imposed on you the stereotyped image of a sweet girl, thereby also losing whatever assertive and creative mana qualities you possess. Responsibility for undermining is about equally divided between you for carrying role-playing concepts out of bed *where they do not belong, unless that is mutually agreed upon.* I say to you in particular, that as you conceive it—THERE IS NO SUCH THING AS A *MAN.* And I say to him, as he conceives it—BOYS ARE NOT *GIRLS.* When belief to the contary is heavy in the air between you—when those delusions are paramount, you are both heading for the rocks.

Q. You don't know the butches I've known.

A. My dear, I've known butches from Ogunquit, Maine, to Mexico City, from Montreal to New Orleans—and over a good part of Europe. As you conceive it, THERE IS NO SUCH THING AS A MAN. The type of guys you hang your fantasy on may look butch and act tough but by and large they are self-deceived and lost children in the world. You have yet to learn —and I would like you to think about this—that your butches may have muscles and be good at a bar scrap or pasting you one, but—like the justified targets of the women's liberation movement—they are not real men. *Real masculinity has to do with effectiveness in terms of competing in the real world.* It has to do with winning adversary-system battles in occupational arenas where your butch would fall with step one; it has to do with fighting an inner battle for self-identity—such as the one you are fighting right now as you try to understand yourself and how to please your partner as a sensuous homosexual human being. That's manliness! And it is that sort of manliness that *you tend to overlook* in your partner, while *imposing the delusion* of the other sort of so-called manliness upon him. A cold cream jar, indeed!

Q. You feel strongly about this.

A. I do. And I apologize for speaking so emphatically and peremptorily. You are not alone in entertaining that delusion of manliness. Nor is your partner alone in entertaining the delusion that because you submit to him in bed you are really a girl. Have your dominant and submissive illusions in bed, where they work, but out of bed begin to see each other as struggling and developing human beings. On that basis, love can truly begin to create its wonders between you.

Q. Do I need it? I mean love to create wonders . . .

A. Yes, you do. Aloneness is no great tragedy, it's a time to repair your soul and prepare it for what you have planned ahead. But to be lonely, by which I mean, all alone permanently, robs you of a warm and broad undergirding in your life so vital for producing *anything*. The more I get to know effective people, the more I see how *a bracing background of devotion has been the spawning ground for whatever it is they are or have produced.* And I mean *someone at home who cares*, who will listen, whose own eye on reality is sharp, who provides the check-and-balance system for excess of zeal or for those terrible times of self-doubt. When gay lovers get that kind of fulcrum relationship rolling——and they can if they try—there is no stopping the miracles they can accomplish together or separately. The life of each of them, then, is steeped always in delight, power and, sometimes, even glory.

Q. I'd like to ask you about infidelity.

A. I'm yours, ask.

Q. I have been unfaithful to my lover. Sometimes I've told him, sometimes not. I always feel terrible.

A. Then don't do it anymore.

Q. I can't help it.

A. Yes, I understand, unfaithfulness in gay life is a prevalent problem. You really do love your lover; you have exchanged actual or tacit vows of loyalty. But someone crosses your path and you find him irresistible, and there is a convenient opportunity for consummation. It happens, just happens. And you return to your lover, whom you do love, and you're upset with yourself. I think that in our changing and permissive world we have learned to be frank with ourselves, if with no one else, about the *way it is*. So, taking a cue from that, I'd say, *do it and forget it. Completely.* Never even hint at it with your lover when you're in that

perverse, provocative mood that overcomes you at such times. Be
a man, in the best sense of that word, and have the courage to
keep your own counsel. I'm told of a Russian proverb that defines
a hero as a man who can resist his own smart remark. Be a hero
like that and block your impulse to tell your lover and imply that
somehow he fails you. Go on with your life with your lover and
pray that you are not too often put to the test. Keep in mind that
the day may dawn when your lover cheats and somehow you find
out; believe then that it is as possible for him to trick out and still
love you, as it was for you to have done so. About your lover's
tricking out: the effect of it may be a backlash in your favor. The
chances are a quickie on his part (or on yours) will be only a
mediocre experience and lead him to appreciate *you*, the person
he's got, all the more. Or, reassured by the experience outside of
his attractiveness, he'll come back to you feeling more worthy of
you. Clouds do have silver linings. If he tricks out too frequently
you'd better hurry up and discover what it is you are not giving
him instead of worrying about what he's going after. And supply
it, fast.

Q. May I ask one last question?

A. Certainly.

Q. How do you handle a break-up?

A. I handle it as miserably as anyone else. But there are certain
things you can do *by rote*, since, during a break-up, meaning
goes out of life. *First, don't try to stifle your grief*; admit it and
ride with it, express it to friends, and at midnight let the tears run
into your ears, as Edna St. Vincent Millay advised. *Second*, you
will compulsively relive the good times and the bad—so while
you're at it, examine the circumstances; try to understand what
went wrong. Drink the cup to its bitterest dregs: accept responsibility when it was yours, assign it to him when you truly believe it
was his. *Third*, attempt to establish for yourself simple routines
away from your job as well as throwing yourself into the routines
at your job. Routines can get you across the hours, and time-

—between now and when you broke up—is what you are playing for, so that the hurt can heal. For me, the worst hour is after work, near sunset, and I have accepted not a little help from my friends to survive it. *Fourth*, remember that at some point suffering turns into ideas, and when it does, your Phoenix of rebirth will rise from the ashes. After a break-up, I like to believe that I showed courage to love at all. And I like to believe that I stand with William Faulkner, who ended his novel, The Wild Palms, with this sentence: "Between grief and nothing, I will take grief."

Q. That is a great sentence, and I understand it. Thank you for answering my questions.

A. Glad to. But let's part on a lighter note. Dorothy Parker, a woman who loved and suffered, was never at a loss for her wit. Here's how she handled the problem of keeping lovers:

In youth, it was a way I had
To do my best to please,
And change, with every passing lad,
To suit his theories.
But now I know the things I know,
And do the things I do;
And if you do not like me so,
To hell, my love, with you.

15

YOU AND YOUR QUICKIES!

What is important for you to realize about your partner in a quickie is that he wants it quick! Time is the crucial element here—and there is no time for the rococo blow job you're famous for. Even if you have him in a john standing in a shopping bag (people looking under the door of the booth will see only one pair of feet), you've got to hurry or someone's gonna get wise. Slurping noises kept to a minimum. Just have him whip it out and go, baby, go!—so fast that your hair flies, your necklace gets turned around and he's zipping up before you can say Michael York (you wish). Haste makes waste of what might have been, but remember: a bird in the hand in the john is worth two in the bushes outside!

The nugget of excitement about quickies is the anonymity of the experience, and as I said, the speed with which it is accomplished. Again, I have to laugh at straights and their momentous discovery through Marlon Brando in "Last Tango In Paris" that anonymous sex can be fun: a gay ploy for untold centuries; a piece of information that the variest go-go boy in L. A. imbibed with his first trick's come. Ah, well, give them time . . .

The delicious outer shell of excitement about quickies is the *place where*. Now we're on to something. I want to remind you that there is no prohibition against you and your longtime lover taking advantage of the suggestions I'm going to offer you about transient tricking. The sky is *no* limit when it comes to quickies. (Anyone who isn't a member of the five-mile-high club—jumbo jet john jobs—go the rear of the class: old stuff, not much challenge.)

Truck or car rest stop areas along super-highways are a fine new field—as new as the highway itself. I have a friend, his nickname is Brownie, who makes an art of cruising rest stops. I'm not going to take you through it in detail except to say that Brownie says you've got to butch it up and at the same time swish so that the truck drivers (not overly subtle) do not really believe you woke them to ask for a match. It's a narrow line. And you must be ready to spring out of the cab if the driver is surly. Usually, Brownie says, they're rather grateful, and Brownie has a few old faithfuls who think of him as one more facility of the stop, like the candy machine or the john. Brownie is enraged at this new practice of certain Women's Lib-conscious drivers who travel with their wives in the cab! Is no male enclave to retain exclusivity, Brownie pleads.

Dune or bullrush quickies are still popular. Adjunctive to beach cruising, dune cruising means action: a gay mountain-climbing instinct bodying forth. Surely to caroom over those dry, hot and windswept dune requires grit; retaining your foothold on a sand precipice while manipulating someone else's penis is a complicated feat. Or you may join the dune-sitters (what good is sitting alone in your dune?) who contemplate for hours and hours—possibly yogi—until Mr. Right strolls into view, and then it's a mad scramble to see which of you will qualify for the stroller. Many are called but few are chosen to make out. The etiquette of bullrush or forest-glade cruising along the little winding, cloven-hoof-marked paths isn't too rigorous. You mustn't mind a branch or two slapping across your face. Watching from a five-foot distance isn't discouraged, but closer is bad form. It is my personal fancy that enchanted forests across the milleniums (Fairies at the bottom of our garden) became "enchanted" for common folks by just such gay carryings-on. Oh, I'd better warn you—the self-same little paths at night are hosts often to bands of disgruntled townies who didn't get laid by day, and who are most inhospitable to persons caught there after dark.

I regret to say that *truck van quickies* (yes, in the van part of a parked truck) are in. It wonders me that anyone cares to participate; the vans are malodorous with pee and even a dump or two. Still, the attraction is there, especially after the bars close. It's very much like oysters, an acquired taste, I suppose, and I mean no derogation of oysters, which I like immensely. But suppose the truck driver should appear! And suppose the van should trundle off, the driver all unaware of his fornicating passengers! Imagine their surprise at starting to suck in Manhattan and finishing in Pennsylvania: pandemonium! Across state lines—there may even be a law!! No thank you.

Then there are the *usual unusual places*: fitting rooms in stores, on the plane to P-town, on the boat from the coast to Nantucket, in the abandoned gun emplacements on Fishers Island, behind the war monuments of so many small town squares, in your building basement laundry-room closet, in the sleigh seat of a merry-go-round, in a Karmen Ghia (smaller than a Beetle), on the pool terrace of the Caribe-Hilton in San Juan with one of those brass-buttoned waiters who crouch-fuck your elbow while you give your order, in the dentist's chair waiting for the novocaine to take effect, or after the novocaine has taken effect, on the parachute jump at Atlantic City, in the baptistry while you and your cousin wait for his mother with the baby, in a parking space, preferably in a car newer and larger than yours (Rolls Royces are divine—all that leather and fine-grained wood give the moment a tone), at the opening of an art gallery where everyone is jammed in and holding drinks (also rather tony)—and so many other spots. Use the space on the rest of this page to note your own favorites.

16

POPPERS, POT, PILLS, POPPY PARTS AND PINK LADIES–APHRODISIACS?

The question is: Is there anything mentioned in the title of this chapter that you can inhale, ingest or inject that is going to improve your sex life?

Let's start out by saying that the buzzin', bloomin' drug scene of '67, '68, '69, is gone. A mind-bending trip for a lot of people, it did result in souvenirs. Art directors discovered different color spectrums, and thanks to the Beatles' "Yellow Submarine," cartoonishness had a vogue. Fabric designers were inspired; mystic prophets came into their own. The young benefited most: blowing your mind was a fast way of cleaning out middle-class clichés and growing up instanteously. Expanded consciousness was the order of the day, and not a bad order.

Still, Aldous Huxley's book "Doors of Perception" led us less to a temple or a garden than to drug-therapy halfway houses. I thought the flower child's gesture of planting a posie in a gun barrel touching, but the guns continued, as we witnessed at Kent State. And in Vietnam.

The era and the transition period are epitomized for me by the life of a former lover. He went from preppy to hippie in three busy months. As a hippie, he zonked himself with half a hundred LSD applications. He was strong enough to avoid the fate of his LSD compatriots who ended up in mental institutions (one unforgettable hippie friend of my lover is still in one; he believes he is an orange). But my ex- did not facilitate by drugs his talent as an actor; and he did have several close calls with the law. Today, I am glad to report—for I loved him, and do still—he has found himself as a lecturer in the service of a popular guru. I've seen him once since his conversion, and he looks beautiful—but he always did to me. The era helped many of the young find their spiritual attributes much more than it helped them to discover anything new about themselves sexually. Unless you reason that a raised and expanded consciousness is in itself liable to liberate sexually.

If you took drugs and became gay, you probably would have become gay anyhow (though it may have rushed the process). I doubt if it radically altered sexual preference. If it had, we would have heard. Our ranks would stretch to the moon.

Everyone who tripped (banana skins, I remember, were the rage at one point) found out that, yes, the mind has greater dimensions than one had known. And also, there were more incisive methods of achieving relaxation than swallowing two Bufferin. Or taking a martini. Or two. As for an *aphrodisiac propellent*—prognosis negative in regard to most drugs.

For the record, let's look over the field.

Poppers

The only drug to materially and immediately affect sexual performance. A convenient bedside popper has heightened many a climax. A kick in the heart—and intended as you know, for heart sufferers—poppers facilitate mega-orgasm; come gushing rather than dribbling out, accompanied by racing pulse and-

—presumably—racy enjoyment of the act. I have wondered what my response would be if I were screwing someone who took a popper to climax and expired instead. Would I go ahead and have my orgasm? I think I might. Business is business.

Pot and Hash

Pot was one of the great discoveries of the era—and a beneficial one. It has the happy faculty of slicing through the mind's accumulated sludge of fear, guilt, and middle-class values (*mistakenly* equated with integrity) and causing a receptivity of mind surprising and helpful to hidebound folks. Relaxed and diverted from obsessive-compulsive Puritanism, the psyches of large numbers of people were *freed for sex*. And their bodies did not have to take the beating that goes with subsisting on martini olives or lemon peel, or manhattan cherries.

I was turned on to hash before being introduced to pot. In the mid sixties I didn't much smoke even cigarettes. A thoughtful friend, who is an excellent pop pianist, had a special hash party for about ten of us gay solid citizens of a resort town who, like myself, did not smoke. He did the neighborly thing: he baked gingerbread cookies, à la Alice B. Toklas. We all knew the cookies were laced, and we wanted to try them. I thought—and I believe the others did—it would be another form of cocktail party where you go for a pleasant hour of bitchery and conniving, thank your host and repair to dinner. I had made an engagement with someone for dinner at eight. I arrived at my friend's place at six-thirty, the others arrived, the cookies were proferred—like holy wafers, I thought—and I partook, glanced at my watch and saw it was nine-thirty! Also, curiously, the others were either gyrating to music inaudible to me or lying about pulseless. My own head was fine, escept that if I tried to turn it I was sure that it would keep turning 360 degrees. To my chagrin, my host said he did not believe that I should drive my own car but that it would be wiser to go to dinner with several others at the party who were leaving then. Ruffled, since I somehow had lost track of events, including my dinner-at-eight date with a person I couldn't recall, I was ushered into a strange car with people who were only vaguely familiar to me. We did get to a restaurant, the food was exceptionally tasty, but the people I was with became increasingly less familiar. Until I realized that I was a Russian commissar interviewing these people for jobs teaching high-school behind the Iron Curtain. When I awoke the next morning, in my own bed, I felt marvelous, and I had a memorable bowel movement and not the least idea where my car was.

Uppers And Downers

The facts are: uppers *put you up* and your driving verbal personality bespeaks an active sex life to whomever you're cruising. Bedtime, however, is liable to *show you up* without much credit to the erotic line you talked beforehand. Downers put you way down so that listening to the juke box and grooving on the bright and responsive crowd around you in a bar become your preoccupations. If a misguided person sees depth in the impression you give of "still water," and you do get him home, the sex scene can be lengthy. What you lack in get-away you'll compensate for in endurance. End story of the effect of pseudo-scientifically brand-named drugs on your psyche and, inadvertently, your sex life.

It all began—for the most part—during World War II when a weary foot soldier standing night guard duty wished out loud that there was a pill he could take that would keep him alert. And later, in his grimy bunk, a pill that would short-circuit anxiety and let him sleep. Didn't science just jump to the challenge! And take us along for the ride!

My own observation about speed pills, and pills containing speed-plus, is that words flow without effort: pill talk. I've noticed that one loses correct estimation—or any conception—of effect: hard lines on a writer whose stock-in-trade is creating emotional effects with words. Words come to hand, but they do not grip; the effect is of oneself talking to oneself only. Language used to relieve anxiety is one-dimensional, disingenuous, absurd.

LSD

For sex? Old pros might say yes, but the majority of my head friends dissent. Strictly private. Mind-movies. Do not disturb till the show is over (certainly no one admitted toward the end). My lover-turned-mystic was something of an LSD authority-in-residence that winter. He used it less and less, though. We decided one spring night I should try it. I felt queasy first (perfectly natural he assured me); then very queasy; then the walls began to ripple (doing fine, he said); then there was a fuzzy spider inside my head bumping against the inside of my cranium (par for the course, he told me, yawning); then I began to scream and yell at him, asking for reiteration of his love for me and for reassurance that he wouldn't ever leave me (he'd fallen asleep); I was convinced that I'd blown a fuse in my physiological electrical system and that my heart would stop. I woke him and he said it wouldn't and he went to bed. Colors and surfaces were still trembling suspiciously the next afternoon. But I'd come down. As my lover left to shop, he asked me how I felt. I thought he really should have been able to tell by my deep eye sockets, my broken manner. "You had a mild trip," he said. "I'll get better stuff next time."

Heroin, Cocaine, Morphine.

If pot is the great lady of the drug world, these three are the evil sisters, too cruel even to joke about. Aphrodisiacs? No. I have seen on the street the lowering and transfixed eyes: the zombie walk. I have faced an addict as a night intruder in my apartment. He'd come through a porch window and when I woke up he was standing by my bed. Chilling. I split with him the money I had in my wallet and kissed him for good luck. (He became known around the resort town as the kissing bandit.) When it comes to the serious drug-takers, I am impressed not with their individuality, but with the alikeness of their talk and their modes of talking. High, one junkie resembles another; as if they were comforming to a vast archetype; as if, high, they had found a community of man where they belonged—felt comfortable, without pain.

*   *   *   *

(Patton's Slap)

I'd like to tell you the following story because it puts the drug world—and other worlds, as you'll see—in a light so harsh it made me angry. I hope it angers you, and I heartily wish a junkie or two could hear it—it might make them angry enough to think. I found the anger salutary: I hope you do.

A few summers ago, I entered into an agreement with a lady to assist her editorially in the writing of her memoirs. She is one of the richest and most social and most vigorous grande dames in the country. And honey, I mean super-rich. (Super-rich never meant much to me until I saw it parsed out that summer.) She owns a mansion on Long Island, an apartment on Park Avenue, a plantation in North Carolina, (19,000 acres), a ranch in Colorado (over 200,000 acres), houses in London, Paris and the French Riviera town of Antibes, stables at Saratoga and her own plane, which she flies herself, to get from place to place. I unconscionably adored all of that part. The grande dame is famous for her big-game hunting, and her specimens are on display at many natural history museums.

I tell you all this to set the background of the scene. The scene itself is at her mansion on Long Island, in a two-story, wood-paneled and candle-lit dining room.where she presides at a table of forty dinner guests—one of her lesser crowds. The men and women at the table are people of her own financial distinction: mostly old, and a very grimly rightist group. The lady—let's call her Vida—has had, before dinner, three orange tigers (vodka, rocks, with a twist of orange: tigers are her personal symbol) and, with dinner, wine. She is gassed. And when she's gassed, look out! She's touchy—and *filled with monologue*. Her monologue that night was set off by a chance remark about the use of drugs' becoming more prevalent in this country. Vida has wide-apart, flashing eyes, a mouth downturned like a shark's and her voice is a much-used trowel. Her monologue went like this:

"I've seen 'em, dope fiends on the street, *most unattractive*. Seen 'em in Indo-China, now Vietnam, where I went after tiger in '32. Saw the coolies lying around in their dens . . . You know what I think, I think *good riddance* . . . and the same about the junkies here who, for my money, are just the same as the coolies there. Whole class of people, millions in China even today . . . looking at the pictures in their heads . . . so let 'em, I say . . . nobody wants that trash . . . *we certainly don't want 'em in our world* . . . all that dumb lingo and standing around in doorways . . . they make a whole life of it. They don't have any other life . . . and they don't deserve any . . . people who shouldn't have been born in the first place . . . *Patton was right* when he slapped down that soldier . . . same idea . . . malingers, fakers, junk they are, junk they should have . . . a humane way to exterminate 'em . . . can't cope, too anxious, they whine. Hell, we're all anxious. . . . except for thievery dope makes 'em impotent . . . useless bodies . . . haven't a chinaman's chance for life . . . and I guess those words first meant the chinese coolie . . . and the dope friends here are exactly *like 'em* . . . good for living in doorways and dying in doorways . . . mostly blacks . . . wetbacks . . . puerto ricans . . . the hell with 'em if they want the stuff, give it to 'em free . . . put's 'em out of the way . . . the fags have sex, talking about it or doing it keeps them quiet . . . now if we could only figure out a way to handle the jews . . .''

I don't want to leave you with a wholly negative impression of Vida. Each year, her great charity donation is money for the upkeep of a gorilla preserve in Kenya. No, her book never got written.

*   *   *

Booze

I don't suppose I have to explain booze, or defend it. By chance, could it be that you've led so sheltered a life that you've never ever tried a dry martini? I thought not. Hemingway said taking a drink was the only way to end a day. Let's call booze the axle grease of the world that love makes go round. Entering a party or bar, you may not see a soul with even a shred of mana to attract you. After two drinks, a few individuals you had earlier dismissed seem Possibles now. After the third drink, those few then seem exceedingly attractive. That's how booze works for me. Unfortunately, *the next morning* the trick I chose from among the few is back to what he looked like to me in the first place. Ah well: I had my one white singing hour of peace.

The nice thing about booze is bars. If pot only had the convivial and convenient dealership system that booze has, it might take hold.

Unless you're a solitary drinker—and I am occasionally: I like my cocktail whether there's anyone around or not—booze does *join* people. I can hear the shrieks from the pot lobby. Yes, but one is prone to *chat* more with shiny manhattan in hand than one is with the ineffable joint. Pot joins people, but more in *silent communication*; just as *valid*, I grant you, but somehow less cheery. It really is more difficult to be smilingly, deliciously bitchy stoned than it is to be that way three sheets to the wind.

The solution, of course, is to stand at a party with a drink in one hand and a joint in the other.

Summary

The answer to the question posed at the start—whether any of the various drugs you can inhale, ingest or inject has aphrodisiac potency—is: not really. The effect of some or all of these things may be to jazz up *your* sex life, but it's an individual reaction.

As to the sexual efficacy of nutmeg, vitamin C or E, oysters, emu eggs, shark fins, cobra, avocados, squid (sautéed), robins' brains, boll weevil excreta, lizards' toes, PABA, spanish fly (an irritant to membranes merely), ambergris or eye of newt—I admit my research is incomplete. I have found that a thick steak, rare, often as not turns the trick—if you feed it to him!

17

TO ORGY OR NOT TO ORGY

I like orgies. But then, I have night-eyes; I see well in the dark. I hope you like orgies (night-eyes aren't necessary). When I am "at orgy," I have a feeling of connection with ancient Greece or Rome (where they certainly knew how to throw an orgy). You may feel it too. True, orgies can have *unfavorable aspects*, but I shall show you *how to avoid them*, and *how to enjoy yourself*.

If you're giving an orgy, here are a few, simple, common-sense things to do: make sure the floor space is uncluttered (put that antique chair in the kitchen)—there'll be action on the floor. It is wise to spread a coverlet or two and lots of pillows, prefera-bly washable. Lighting is important: low and infrequent spots of illumination. Music is indispensible; arrange a variety of selec-tions. With music at orgies, as with so much else in gay life, variety is the spice. Unfortunately in gay life, variety is for some also the meat and drink, and never more so than at an orgy. I have, at my orgies, found that a light snack is good to keep on hand and always ready. Drinks, must flow, and pot glow. *Try not to use the same tray that you used for the pot and drink parapher-*

nalia for the various lubricants you will offer; in the dark at an orgy, people get mixed up and put anything in their mouths. Imagine choking on a tube of KY!

An orgy is fun! Tell yourself this no matter if you're going to or giving one. *It is not dirty*; embroilment has a cleansing effect. *It is not crazy*; people as eminently sane as you are will be there along with you. *It is not dangerous* in terms of the police—if they come they'll say turn down the music; invite them to join in (they've been known to accept). *It doesn't take long*; or if it does, that's because you'll be enjoying yourself so much—grappling among all those hot, meaty, bodies.

As the *host* you will be expected *to lead* the parade. It's a good idea for your guests to disrobe as soon as they arrive; that saves everybody from the kittenish routine of sitting around and daring some else to go first. Guide them to a seat (it'll be dark, don't forget), hand them a drink—and your host duty is done. Only then, they'll see *you're* bare!

As *a guest*, you are expected—as at any party—*to mingle*, and, especially at orgies, to be *kind*. Let the old gentleman have his moment or two (I said *kind, not generous*—if you begin like that, you won't last an hour!) with *your* gorgeous body; you'll feel ready to burst when Mr. Right confronts you in the darkness. Stay away from beauties who upstage each other. Get where the action is. Soon you'll be climbing the stairway to paradise! If you drop a glass, and it breaks, you have a moral duty to report it.

Orgies: In Favor

1. You'll find *not* that you're not presentable, but that you're in demand! If you've tended to your exercise system (remember?), you're body is in fine shape and your aura will shine even in the dark. You will also discover (and it's relieving) that the best-looking men have a little paunch when they aren't delib-

erately holding it in, and that you shouldn't have been worried about yours for one minute. Observe that twenty-year-old on all fours: his sagging tummy makes him look like a pregnant cat. What are they doing to him anyway . . . just go and see.

2. If, as either host or guest, you bring your lover, and he has sex with someone (or a number of someones) you can hardly accuse him of being unfaithful or deceitful—since you're one of his someones! It is the ultimate in sharing. A wonderful way to rev up your relationship; when you get home, you can play "orgy" and re-enact the whole scene with *you* doing all the parts!

3. If you haven't a lover, and go by yourself to an orgy, it's a chance to break that hoop of iron that's been around your emotions. Let go, let it all hang out; everyone will adore you for it. You, indeed, may *make* the party—everybody. As important as is the process in life of finding yourself, there's a time in life when it is equally important to lose yourself. Orgies are the perfect opportunity, with more than one sexual experience to envelope you. Realize every fantasy!

4. Orgy rooms have a strange appeal. The atmosphere of an orgy is far from wordless, but if it's a good and busy orgy there is a hushed and sanctified mood in the orgy room. A venerable human rite is being performed and it commands your attention, if not respect. (I admit I feel the same thing at the Continental steam baths, or fuck movies. Incidently, they've improved the scenic design in those movies; the last one I saw showed two males having sex and by the bed there was a *bowl of roses*.) Back at the orgy: surely what I feel of the sanctity of a good orgy is that historical connection I mentioned earlier. They did the same things in Greece and Rome. Has civilization marched ahead?

5. The purport of this book has been to re-awaken your senses, and to impress upon you that you're a desirable sexual being. An orgy is the place where you can be *purely a sexual being*. And you're perfectly safe. Nobody is going to put any ties on you if

you don't want them. Or reproach you for what you did or didn't do. Or blame you for being greedy. It sounds like a nice place to live.

6. To participate, you need not strain your wardrobe allowance for a new outfit.

Orgies: Not In Favor

1. At an orgy, it is de rigeur to mingle—you can't make a conquest and then take your meat to eat in a corner. It's not done. If you try it, you'll simply be cramped in a corner with lots of people instead of in the middle of the room with lots of people where everyone would have been more comfortable.

2. If you bring your lover and for an instant lose track of him —then see he's the center of attention under the piano, that scene may come back to you in jealous nightmares. Especially if *they're* doing it to him in a way he would never allow *you* to do it to him. Slide over there and check on what's happening.

3. If you're a romantic, as I am, orgies may damp down your spirit. Someone may say, "Thanks, that was great," but an orgy is not the place for more lyrical expression. And if you do find someone with whom you are excessively compatible and who tends to your needs with a fervor you hadn't known for some while, you are liable to experience real remorse when he leaves you and you watch him carry on exactly the same way with someone else. You've fallen in love, but he's simply enjoying himself. Now, now, no murmuring to yourself, "I thought we had something special"—against the rules, and he didn't have a good profile anyway, you think.

4. Orgies always have a few clinkers. These are people who are bound and determined to have their way with you in a direction you don't go, have no interest in going, will never go—then suddenly you're excited and boom! you're off! And chagrined. *And surprised at you*. Rise, and go to where they're serving

drinks, or pot, and take five. Return to the rough and tumble and do it to somebody the way it was done unto you! This is known as the orgiast's revenge. Every party has a clinker. Then watch him gleefully as *he* gets up and goes to the bar!

5. I suppose the most severe anti-orgy indictment is that you can at an orgy catch a communicable disease—venereal, various rashes, or hepatitis. Not even attempted blackmail for being at an orgy matches getting sick. Your safeguard against this is to know the host and trust in his choice of people. On the other hand, everybody has a better time if one guest is not well known, or known at all, to the others. This is where it helps to have those night-eyes. If you're in doubt, persuade the number you like to go with you to the bar, where there is usually some light, and inspect him. If he asks you what you're doing when you look in his mouth or ask him to take a deep breath or tell him to spread his cheeks—say you're taking a course in anatomy and his is the best example you've seen. If, in two weeks, your night-eyes turn a fetching hepatitic yellow, you know you failed the course.

6. Orgies can plunge you into conflict. You can become addicted to orgies, and at the same time be afflicted by a demonic nervousness which prevents your expressing yourself at any given orgy. There is only one cure. Find the outdoor spot in your town (which corresponds to behind the monument at Provincetown, or among the low trees at the end of the boardwalk in Cherry Grove), the outdoor spot, to repeat, where orgies are not *given* but simply *occur* when the bars close! At those orgies everyone is an addict like yourself, and exceedingly nervous. Express!

So much for orgies.

I do want to say a word or two about the mini-orgy or, as they're called among the cognoscenti, sandwiches, or threesomes. Like fist penetration, the practice of threesomes is in vogue, especially among longtime lovers. A transient trick is agreed upon by both lovers while they're still at the bar, he is mutually propositioned, acts surprised, accepts a few drinks and returns home in a cab seated between the lovers, ultimately to be sandwiched (whence comes the term) between them in bed. Is it possible for true lovers to share a third person in bed? Who gets what? Is everybody happy? Well, you may not be, but if that's the only method by which you and your lover can survive as a team, vive le troisième, I say!

18

YOU–AND YOUR ORGASM

Now that you've become a sensuous homosexual human being (cum laude) and you're on your way to becoming a super-sensuous one, I believe your sex life will prove far more meaningful and satisfying than it's ever been. I cannot guarantee that you won't, from time to time, suffer a shrewd repulse, but I'll bet your turn-downs are fewer—and that you are able to handle them with grace! Most importantly, you're aware of what it takes to fulfill your partner's needs; you know how to make his experience in bed with you *the most sensational he's ever had*.

The next thing in your order of priorities is *your orgasm*. Oddly, I want to speak first of the times in bed when you may have to *fake it*. After all I've said about being true and real! But I'm also a pragmatist. You may be attracted to your partner very much but find that in the act of anal penetration you just *can't* come. While faking it is almost impossible in oral penetration, your orgasm when penetrating him anally *is* possible to fake, and in my estimation it is wise sometimes to do so. Why? Because *your satisfaction* sexually *does mean a great deal* to your partner;

if he feels he cannot induce it, he takes it as a put-down of his sexual prowess, and though the hurt isn't always obvious, it is deep. You must spare him. The few minutes and few motions it takes to fake it are easier than long explanations as to why you couldn't come (liquor, pot, fatigue, a toothache), which never sound convincing. Fake it!

When faking it is the last thought in your mind, your orgasm should be the symbolic union of yourself not only *with your partner, but with the whole universe!* No less an expression of yourself will do: passion incarnate at climax, and proximity to the living, flaming, heart of reality. You will recognize an at-oneness with all people and all things: the experience is rare but definite. You understand much without having to be told. You feel a sense of flow in yourself and in human existence, and you feel you're borne along by it: at once connected, yet distinct. Afterward, walking with him, perhaps, no matter if the view is of buildings and fire escapes or of clouds and wide beaches—you will find your world is charged with grandeur.

Peace.

19

YOU–AND HIS ORGASM

His moment of orgasm is supreme for him. And so it must be for you. When he comes, you receive the most essential symbol of his being.

About simultaneous orgasm: in theory, great; in practice, an acrobatic stunt. I'm not a stickler for it; I believe something is lost. It deprives each partner, I feel, of the intense concentration on his own climax which gives fullest enjoyment. So—one after the other is best. Save simultaneity for Sundays.

When your partner is about to come, attend him with selfless constancy, even if you are choking, or your beating arm is about to cramp, or you can feel his penis entering your upper intestine. Stick with it! Sounds funny—and these extremities of participation by you are reached—but I mean it. At his moment of climax, *his world is you*, and you cannot and would never want to fail him. *You are also his* at that moment—total felicity. No room here for privity of heart; meld with him to make his orgasm complete.

Strange, how we always remember the people we've had sex

with, if it's only a glimmer of memory. A slender bond exists, though you may see the individual infrequently, just a nod or a smile. And for those you don't ever see again, the bond still exists: even quickies return to us in dreams.

Peace.

20
READY, WILLING, AND SUPER-SENSUOUS!

I dub you Super-Sensuous Homosexual Human Being and award you your degree of Master of Sex!

In this book, you've learned how to *recall yourself to life* by stimulating all five senses, particularly your tactile sense, so important to your enjoyment of sex. There is a deep psychological validity in getting ''right'' with your body—it's a practical way of getting ''right'' with your emotions and then with your mind. Don't you think it's close to what Wilde meant when he said, ''Nothing but the senses can cure the soul''?

You've learned that if that interior of yours is in harmony with itself you'll be in harmony with other people, and that among them will be some you will want to go to bed with. And believe me, they'll be eager to get to bed with you—and not just once! *Sensuous people possess a secret of living and loving* that is irresistible, and it has little to do with looks or youth or cash. It does have to do with *consciously appreciating and enjoying the fact that you're alive:* taking care of yourself physically, not being afraid, developing your aura, grasping the concept of mana and the gay theory of relativity—and believing that there are people in the world who are waiting to love you and be loved by you.

As to that, you have learned how to drive your lover to ecstasy, and how to keep a particular lover once you have him.

You have traveled the highways and byways of drugs and booze as aphrodisiacs; you've been shown of the delights and drawbacks of orgies.

You have learned to cherish your partner's orgasm as well as your own.

But I am beset by two apprehensions.

First, by things you should know about gay life that I haven't had the space to mention (and which knowledge would result in your earning your final degree as Doctor of Sex). Subjects such as:

The eroticism of elegance and the eroticism of trashiness; the loose categories of "types" that gay people fall into; the fascinating field of gay sexual ethics; and the equally fascinating field of transsexuality (our own Christine Jorgenson now has a British counterpart in Jan Morris); the special problems pretty boys must contend with (and the problems of their admiring slaves).

I wanted to describe to you the delightful art of our famous drag entertainers, particularly Arthur Blake, who can take a listless Sunday-afternoon gay crowd in Provincetown and shape it into a howling-with-laughter audience with just a hat or a boa, or a different haircomb; I wanted to cover the difficult but urgent subject of gay hustlers and straight hustlers hustling gays; and the provocative subject of a gay's relationship with his parents—how to maintain and improve it; the extremely relevant subject of gay organizations, doing so much to help and free gay people; the dangers of fag hags; whether or not there's a Gay Mafia in control of jobs in certain fields; I wanted to examine the charge that homosexuality is a "security disease"; I wanted to look into the changes in campus life since gay and active campus associations came into being; and the subject of how West Coast gay life affects us all.

I hope to handle these subjects, and more, in a future book.

My other apprehension?

Have I said enough about gay love? Have I described the mystical illumination that bursts upon you and your friend? Fantastic! Both of you see clearly the world as it is. Care for it. Enjoy it. You both also see, or sense, a secret plan. Life for the two of you has meaning as it never had previously. It seems—as you each think back—that the time you spent before you met was barren and wasted. Loving each other, you share a miraculous knowledge of truth and beauty; you are mysteriously in touch with a reality beneath the surface.

I want to say something about gay alliances that last only briefly. I have found, as you may have, that those momentary attractions can be awesome in their brilliance. Desire, passion, tenderness packed into a two-hour relationship—as much emotion as some individuals know in a lifetime! And worth the risk and the sorrow. Sara Teasdale portrayed my feeling in her poem "Barter."

> *Spend all you have for loveliness,*
> *Buy it and never count the cost;*
> *For one white singing hour of peace*
> *Count many a year of strife well lost . . .*

They say that answered prayers are the most difficult to contend with—that is, when you pray and receive exactly what you asked for. I can think of little to compare, though, with the joy of finding precisely the person *you* want, and of finding that you are precisely the person *he* wants! In gay life, such meetings are frequent. Your experience of bliss is eerie and astounding. I have been so ecstatic with a lover—and I'm sure this has happened to you—that I did wonder if I was awake or dreaming, and what I had done to deserve such fulfillment or what punishment I might have to endure to pay for it. But I was awake, and bliss continued; as a sensuous homosexual human being, I loved and was loved entirely. So shall you be.

There is another short poem about love I like. About love overcoming.

> *He drew a circle that shut me out—*
> *Rebel, heretic, thing to flout.*
> *But Love and I had the wit to win;*
> *We drew a circle that took him in.*

All the wonderful things you've heard about love are true. Love finds a way, love changes your outlook, love joins you not only with another human being, but with the best in yourself. Never underestimate the power of love, or yourself as lover.

Love is the sweet wound that heals: it can save you.

Be a lover. Lovers are always winners.

Love.

FULFILLED

You recall Dennis. I opened this book with a few words about him and me in bed together. Well, he's back, and he's in bed with me again.

I'm proud of winning Dennis. He had two people contesting for his love: both men were good-looking, likable and intelligent. Al was rich: he offered Dennis a diamond ring if. . . . *But I won DENNIS! And I did so because I've learned how to be a sensuous homosexual human being.* Dennis, who is intuitive, even psychic, said he perceived I had an aura when he first saw me —my sensual aura! So too, your lover will perceive yours! He lies with me now, his head cradled between my neck and shoulder; we just got home and we're having a last cigarette. It's an early and soft spring night; a breeze, warm and fresh and fragrant, caresses our nude bodies—paradise, wouldn't you say!

"Have you finished your book yet?" he asks.

"Yes."

"Can you tell me now what it's about?"

"It's a little book about gay sex, love and life.

"Really? Wild!"

Dennis nuzzles closer into my neck.

"I think it says a thing or two."

"Funny or serious?"

"It's a spoof of all those 'Sensuous' books, but serious, too."

"Did you mention it's fun to be gay?"

"I believe I gave that impression."

"And did you tell it like it is?"

"I've tried, with humor, to tell the truth."

"Gay life is complicated."

"I've said so, and advised gay people to learn to live with complication."

We kiss, we're getting excited, but Dennis puts his head on my shoulder again.

Giggling, he asks: "Am I in it?"

"Yes. I begin and end with our being in bed together."

"Ooo-woof! You're kidding!"

"Nope."

"Oh my God!"

"Do you mind?"

"No, I'm very proud."

"So am I, Dennis."

We kiss again, and it is an effort to draw back, but we haven't quite finished our cigarettes. His head returns to my shoulder. You would like Dennis: he is gentle.

"Will you put your name on it?"

"Can't urge gays to leave their closets, then withhold my name."

"You've thought about it?"

"Carefully."

"Some people won't speak to you again."

"I know. If they don't speak, they're better lost. I believe my good friends will understand, and then . . . some new people may speak to me."

"I'm sure of it."

"And perhaps my declaration may make it easier for a boy or girl someplace, sometime, to have the courage to be themselves."

"It isn't easy."

"No, it isn't."

"But maybe if you and others declare themselves it will be easier."

"I hope so."

Dennis leans across me—he's so beautiful—to reach the ash tray and put out his cigarette. I put out mine, switch off the lamp. Our legs intertwine, our arms enfold, we kiss. Now if you will excuse me, starting at the back of Dennis's neck, I am going to go on my serendipitor's journey and drive him—and me—to ecstasy.

"I believe in aristocracy . . . Not an aristocracy of power, based on rank and influence, but an aristocracy of the sensitive, the considerate and the plucky. Its members are found in all nations and classes, and through all the ages, and there is a secret understanding between them when they meet. They represent the true human tradition, the one queer victory over cruelty and chaos."

–E. M. Forster:
What I Believe